GRE 4000

JEFF KOLBY

Additional educational titles from Nova Press (available at novapress.net):

- **GRE Prep Course** (624 pages, includes software)
  GRE Math Prep Course (528 pages)
- **GMAT Prep Course** (624 pages, includes software)
  GMAT Math Prep Course (528 pages)
  GMAT Data Sufficiency Prep Course (422 pages)
- **Master The LSAT** (608 pages, includes software & 4 official LSAT exams)
- **The MCAT Physics Book** (444 pages)
  The MCAT Biology Book (416 pages)
  The MCAT Chemistry Book (428 pages)
- **SAT Prep Course** (640 pages, includes software)
  SAT Math Prep Course (404 pages)
- **ACT Math Prep Course** (402 pages)
- **Speaking and Writing Strategies for the TOEFL® iBT:** (394 pages, includes audio CD)
  500 Words, Phrases, and Idioms for the TOEFL® iBT: (238 pages, includes audio CD)
- **Law School Basics:** A Preview of Law School and Legal Reasoning (224 pages)

Copyright © 2016 by Nova Press
Previous editions: 2014, 2011
All rights reserved.

Duplication, distribution, or data base storage of any part of this work is prohibited without prior written approval from the publisher.

ISBN-10: 1–889057–78–9
ISBN-13: 978–1–889057–78–1

9P. O. Box 629023
West Hollywood, CA 90069

Phone: 1-310-275-3513
E-mail: info@novapress.net
Website: www.novapress.net

Contents

ABOUT THIS BOOK 5

THE WORDS 7

TECHNIQUES FOR LEARNING NEW VOCABULARY 103

WORD ANALYSIS 119

TEXT COMPLETIONS 143

About This Book

The GRE tests a surprisingly limited number of words. In the following list, you will find words that occur frequently on the GRE. Granted, memorizing a list of words is rather dry, but it is probably the most effective way to improve your performance on the verbal section.

Over the years, this list of 4000 words has been an invaluable tool for students who have both the time and the determination to wade through it. It's chock-full of words that are prime candidates for the GRE.

Whenever possible, one-word definitions are used. Although this makes a definition less precise, it also makes it easier to remember. Many common words appear in the list of words, but with their less common meanings. For example, the common meaning of *champion* is "winner." A less common meaning for *champion* is to support or fight for someone else. (Think of the phrase "to champion a cause.") This is the meaning that would be used in the list.

As you read through the list of words, mark any that you do not know with a check mark. Then when you read through the list again, mark any that you do not remember with two checks. Continue in this manner until you have learned the words.

There are four types of quizzes interspersed in the word list: Matching, Antonyms, Analogies, and Sentence Completions. The Matching quizzes, review words that were just introduced. All the other quizzes contain words from any part of the list.

THE WORDS

A

a cappella without accompaniment

à la carte priced separately

a priori reasoning based on general principles

aback unexpected, surprised

abacus counting device

abandon desert, forsake

abase degrade

abash humiliate, embarrass

abate lessen, subside

abatement alleviation

abbey monastery

abbreviate shorten

abdicate relinquish power or position

abdomen belly

abduct kidnap

aberrant abnormal

abet aid, encourage (typically of crime)

abeyance postponement

abhor detest

abide submit, endure

abject wretched

abjure renounce

ablate cut away

ablution cleansing

abode home

abolish annul, eliminate

abominable detestable

aboriginal indigenous, native

abortive unsuccessful

abound be plentiful

abreast side-by-side

abridge shorten

abroad overseas

abrogate cancel

abrupt ending suddenly

abscess infected and inflamed tissue

abscond to run away (secretly)

absolve acquit, free from blame

abstain refrain

abstract theoretical, intangible

abstruse difficult to understand

abut touch, border on

abysmal deficient, sub par

abyss chasm

academy school

accede yield, agree

accentuate emphasize

accession attainment of rank

accessory attachment, accomplice

acclaim recognition, fame

acclimate accustom oneself to a climate, adjust

acclivity ascent, incline

accolade applause, tribute

accommodate adapt, assist, house

accomplice one who aids a lawbreaker

accord agreement

accost to approach and speak to someone aggressively

accouter equip, clothe

accredit authorize

accrete grow larger

accrue accumulate

accumulate amass

acerbic caustic, bitter (of speech)

acme summit, zenith

acolyte assistant (usually to clergy)

acoustic pertaining to sound

acquaint familiarize

acquiesce agree passively

acquit free from blame

acrid pungent, caustic, choking

acrimonious caustic, bitter, resentful

acrophobia fear of heights

actuate induce, start

acumen insight

acute sharp, intense

ad nauseam to a ridiculous degree

ad-lib improvise

adage proverb

adamant insistent

adapt adjust to changing conditions

adaptable pliable

addendum appendix, supplement

adduce offer as example

adept skillful

adhere stick to

adherent supporter

adieu farewell

adipose fatty

adjacent next to

adjourn suspend, discontinue

adjudicate judge

adjunct addition

administer manage

admissible allowable

admonish warn gently

ado fuss, commotion

Adonis a beautiful man

adroit skillful

adulation applause, worship

adulterate contaminate, corrupt

adumbration overshadow

advent arrival of something important

adventitious accidental, extrinsic

adversary opponent

adverse unfavorable, opposing

adversity hardship

advise give counsel

advocate urge, support

aegis that which protects, sponsorship

aerial pertaining to the air

aerobics exercise

Quiz 1 (Matching)

Match each word in the first column with its definition in the second column. Answers are on page 101.

1. ABASE
2. ABSTAIN
3. ACOLYTE
4. ABEYANCE
5. ABRIDGE
6. ACCOLADE
7. ACRIMONIOUS
8. ADDUCE
9. ADULATION
10. AEROBICS

A. applause
B. caustic
C. shorten
D. applause
E. assistant
F. postponement
G. refrain
H. exercise
I. degrade
J. offer as example

aesthetic pleasing to the senses, beautiful

affable friendly

affect influence

affectation pretense, showing off

affidavit sworn written statement

affiliate associate

affiliation connection, association

affinity fondness

affix fasten

affliction illness

affluent abundant, wealthy

affray brawl

affront insult

aficionado devotee, ardent follower

afoul entangled, in trouble

aft rear

aftermath consequence

agape wonder

agenda plan, timetable

agent provocateur agitator

aggrandize exaggerate

aggravate worsen

aggregate total, collect

aggressor attacker

aggrieve mistreat

aggrieved unjustly injured

aghast horrified

agile nimble

agitate stir up

agnate related on the father's side

agnostic not knowing whether God exists

agrarian pertaining to farming

agronomy science of crop production

air discuss, broadcast

airs pretension

akimbo with hands on hips

akin related

al fresco outdoors

alacrity swiftness
albatross large sea bird
albino lacking pigmentation
alcove recess, niche
alias assumed name
alibi excuse
alienate estrange, antagonize
alight land, descend, to happen to find a place to rest
allay to reassure
allege assert without proof
allegiance loyalty
allegory fable
allegro fast
alleviate lessen, assuage
alliteration repetition of the same sound
allocate distribute
allot allocate, ration
allude refer to indirectly
ally unite for a purpose
almanac calendar with additional information
alms charity
aloof arrogant, detached
altercation argument
altitude height
alto low female voice
altruism benevolence, generosity
amalgamation mixture

amass collect
ambient surrounding, environment
ambiguous unclear
ambivalence conflicting emotions
ambulatory able to walk
ameliorate improve
amenable agreeable
amend correct
amenities courtesies, comforts
amenity pleasantness
amiable friendly
amid among
amiss wrong, out of place
amity friendship, good will
amnesty pardon
amoral without morals
amorous loving, sexual
amorphous shapeless
amortize pay by installments
amphibious able to operate in water and land
amphitheater oval-shaped theater
amuck murderous frenzy
amulet charm, talisman
amuse entertain
anachronistic out of historical order
anaerobic without oxygen
anagram a word formed by rearranging the letters of another word
analgesic pain-soother

Quiz 2 (Antonyms)

Directions: Choose the word most opposite in meaning to the capitalized word. Answers are on page 101.

1. GRATUITOUS: (A) voluntary (B) arduous (C) solicitous (D) righteous (E) befitting

2. FALLOW: (A) fatuous (B) productive (C) bountiful (D) pertinacious (E) opprobrious

3. METTLE: (A) ad hoc (B) perdition (C) woe (D) trepidation (E) apathy

4. SAVANT: (A) dolt (B) sage (C) attaché (D) apropos comment (E) state of confusion

5. RIFE: (A) multitudinous (B) blemished (C) sturdy (D) counterfeit (E) sparse

6. ABRIDGE: (A) distend (B) assail (C) unfetter (D) enfeeble (E) prove

7. PRODIGAL: (A) bountiful (B) dependent (C) provident (D) superfluous (E) profligate

8. REQUIEM: (A) humility (B) prerequisite (C) resolution (D) reign (E) hiatus

9. METE: (A) indict (B) convoke (C) hamper (D) disseminate (E) deviate

10. SEVERANCE: (A) continuation (B) dichotomy (C) astringency (D) disclosure (E) remonstrance

analogous similar
analogy point-by-point comparison
anarchist terrorist, nihilist
anarchy absence of government, chaos
anathema curse, abomination
anecdote story
aneurysm bulging in a blood vessel
angst anxiety, dread

animadversion critical remark
animated exuberant
animosity dislike
animus hate
annals historical records
annex to attach, to take possession of
annihilate destroy
annotate to add explanatory notes

annul cancel
annular ring-shaped
anodyne pain soothing
anoint consecrate, apply ointment
anomalous abnormal
anonymity state of being anonymous
antagonistic hostile
antagonize harass
antechamber waiting room
antediluvian ancient, obsolete
anthology collection
anthrax disease, bacterium
antic caper, prank
antipathy repulsion, hated
antipodal exactly opposite
antiquated outdated, obsolete
antiquity ancient times
antithesis direct opposite
apartheid racial segregation
apathetic unconcerned, uninterested
apathy indifference
ape mimic
aperture opening
apex highest point
aphasia speechless
aphorism maxim
aplomb poise
apocalyptic ominous, doomed
apocryphal of doubtful authenticity
apoplexy stroke
apostate one who abandons one's faith
apotheosis deification
appall horrify
apparition phantom
appease pacify
appellation title
append affix
apposite apt
apprehensive anxious, worried
apprise inform
approbation approval
apropos appropriate
apt suitable
aptitude ability
aquatic pertaining to water
arbiter judge
arbitrament final judgment
arbitrary tyrannical, capricious
arcane secret, difficult to understand
archaic antiquated
archetype original model, epitome
archipelago group of island
archives public records
ardent passionate
ardor passion
arduous hard
Argonauts gold-seekers, adventurers

argot specialized vocabulary, jargon
aria operatic song
arid dry, dull
aristocrat nobleman
armada fleet of ships
armistice truce
arraign indict
array arrangement
arrears in debt
arrogate seize without right
arroyo gully
arsenal supply, stockpile of weapons
artful skillful, cunning
articulate well-spoken
artifice trick
artless naive, simple
ascend rise
ascendancy powerful state
ascertain discover
ascetic self-denying
ascribe to attribute
aseptic sterile
ashen pale
asinine stupid
askance to view with suspicion
askew crooked
aspersion slander
asphyxiate suffocate
aspirant contestant
aspiration ambition
assail attack
assassin murderer
assent agree
assert affirm
assess appraise
assiduous hard-working
assimilate absorb, integrate
assonance partial rhyme
assuage lessen (pain)
astral pertaining to stars
astringent causing contraction, severe
astute wise
asunder apart, into separate parts
asylum place of refuge
asymmetric uneven
atavistic exhibiting the characteristics of one's forebears
atelier workshop
atoll reef
atomize vaporize
atone make amends
atrophy the wasting away of muscle
attenuate weaken, assuage
attest testify
attire dress
attribute ascribe
attrition deterioration, reduction

Quiz 3 (Matching)

Match each word in the first column with its definition in the second column. Answers are on page 101.

1. ANATHEMA	A.	hard
2. ANNIHILATE	B.	curse
3. ANOMALOUS	C.	gully
4. APATHETIC	D.	suffocate
5. ARCHAIC	E.	antiquated
6. ARDUOUS	F.	destroy
7. ARROYO	G.	abnormal
8. ASPHYXIATE	H.	unconcerned
9. ASTRINGENT	I.	make amends
10. ATONE	J.	causing contraction

atypical abnormal

au courant well informed, chic

audacity boldness

audient listening, attentive

audition tryout

augment increase, supplement

augur predict

august noble, majestic

aura atmosphere, emanation

auspices patronage, protection

auspicious favorable

austere harsh, Spartan

authorize grant, sanction

automaton robot

autonomous self-governing

auxiliary secondary, supportive

avail assistance

avant garde vanguard

avarice greed

avatar incarnation

averse loath, reluctant

avert turn away

avian pertaining to birds

avid enthusiastic

avocation hobby

avouch attest, guarantee

avow declare

avuncular like an uncle

awry crooked

axiom self-evident truth

aye affirmative vote

azure sky blue

B

babbittry smugness

bacchanal orgy, drunken celebration

badger pester

badinage banter

bagatelle nonentity, trifle

bailiwick area of concern or business

baleen whalebone
baleful hostile, malignant
balk hesitate
balky hesitant
ballad song
ballast counterbalance
ballistics study of projectiles
balm soothing ointment
banal trite
bandy exchange
bane poison, nuisance
barbarian savage
bard poet
baroque ornate
barrister lawyer
bask take pleasure in, sun
basso low male voice
bastion fort
bathos sentimentality
batten fasten, board up
battery physical attack
bauble trinket
beatify sanctify
beatitude state of bliss
beckon lure
becoming proper
bedlam uproar
befit to be suitable
beget produce, procreate

begrudge resent, envy
beguile deceive, seduce
behemoth monster
behest command
beholden in debt, obliged
belabor assail verbally, dwell on
belated delayed, overdue
beleaguer besiege
belfry bell tower
belie misrepresent, disprove
belittle disparage
bellicose warlike
belligerent combative
bellow shout
bellwether leader, guide
bemoan lament
bemused bewildered
benchmark standard
benediction blessing
benefactor patron
benevolent kind
benign harmless
bent determined
bequeath will
bequest gift, endowment
berate scold
bereave to rob, to deprive somebody of a love one, especially through death

Quiz 4 (Antonyms)

Directions: Choose the word most opposite in meaning to the capitalized word. Answers are on page 101.

1. HYPOCRITICAL: (A) forthright (B) judicious (C) circumspect (D) puritanical (E) unorthodox

2. VOLUMINOUS: (A) obscure (B) cantankerous (C) unsubstantial (D) tenacious (E) opprobrious

3. FANATICISM: (A) delusion (B) fascism (C) remorse (D) cynicism (E) indifference

4. INTERMINABLE: (A) finite (B) jejune (C) tranquil (D) incessant (E) imprudent

5. ORNATE: (A) Spartan (B) blemished (C) sturdy (D) counterfeit (E) temporary

6. MUTABILITY: (A) simplicity (B) apprehension (C) frailty (D) maverick (E) tenacity

7. VIRULENT: (A) benign (B) intrepid (C) malignant (D) hyperbolic (E) tentative

8. ABSTEMIOUS: (A) timely (B) immoderate (C) bellicose (D) servile (E) irreligious

9. VERBOSE: (A) subliminal (B) myopic (C) pithy (D) dauntless (E) ubiquitous

10. VISCID: (A) subtle (B) faint (C) slick (D) vicious (E) difficult

---

bereft deprived of

berserk crazed with anger

beseech implore, beg

beset harass, encircle

besiege beleaguer, surround

besmirch slander, sully

bespeak attest

bestial beast-like, brutal

bestow offer, grant

betrothed engaged

bevy group

bibliography list of sources of information

bicameral having two legislative branches

bicker quarrel

biennial occurring every two years

bilateral two-sided
bilious ill-tempered
bilk swindle
biodegradable naturally decaying
biopsy removing tissue for examination
biped two-footed animal
bistro tavern, cafe
bivouac encampment
blandish flatter, grovel
blasé bored with life
blasphemy insulting God
bleak cheerless, forlorn
blight decay
bliss happiness
blithe joyous
bloated swollen
bode portend
bogus forged, false
bogy bugbear
boisterous noisy
bolt move quickly and suddenly
bombast pompous speech
bon vivant gourmet, epicure
bona fide made in good faith
bonanza a stroke of luck
boon payoff, windfall
boor vulgar person
bootless unavailing

booty loot, stolen goods
botch bungle
bourgeois middle class
bovine cow-like
boycott abstain in protest
bracing refreshing
brackish salty
brandish display menacingly
bravado feigned bravery
bravura technically difficult, brilliant
brawn strength
brevity shortness of expression
brigand robber
brink edge, threshold
broach bring up a topic for conversation
bromide cliché
brook tolerate
browbeat to bully
brusque curt
bucolic rustic
buffet blow, pummel
buffoon fool, joker
bulwark fortification
buncombe empty, showy talk
buoyant floatable, cheerful
burgeon sprout
burlesque farce
burly husky
buttress support

C

cabal a group of conspirators
cabaret nightclub
cache hiding place
cachet prestige
cacophony dissonance, harsh noise
cadaver corpse
cadaverous haggard
cadence rhythm
cadet a student of a military academy
cadge beg
cadre small group
cajole encourage, coax
calamity disaster
calculating scheming
caliber ability, character
callous insensitive
callow inexperienced
calumny slander
camaraderie fellowship
canaille rabble
canard hoax
candid frank, unrehearsed
candor frankness
canine pertaining to dogs
canon rule
cant insincere speech
cantankerous peevish
cantata musical composition
canvass survey
capacious spacious
capillary thin tube
capital most significant, pertaining to wealth
capitol legislative building
capitulate surrender
capricious fickle, impulsive
caption title
captious fond of finding fault in others
captivate engross, fascinate
carafe bottle
carbine rifle
carcinogenic causing cancer
carcinoma tumor
cardinal chief
cardiologist one who studies the heart
careen swerve
carrion decaying flesh
cartographer mapmaker
cascade waterfall
cashmere fine wool from Asia
Cassandra unheeded prophet
castigate criticize
castrate remove the testicles

Quiz 5 (Matching)

Match each word in the first column with its definition in the second column. Answers are on page 101.

1. BESMIRCH
2. BICAMERAL
3. BILATERAL
4. BOOTLESS
5. BRANDISH
6. BURLESQUE
7. CABAL
8. CANINE
9. CANTANKEROUS
10. CASSANDRA

A. unheeded prophet
B. peevish
C. pertaining to dogs
D. plot
E. farce
F. display menacingly
G. unavailing
H. two-sided
I. having two legislative branches
J. sully

casuistry specious reasoning
cataclysm catastrophe
catastrophic disastrous
categorical absolute, certain
cathartic purgative, purifying
catholic universal, worldly
caucus meeting
cause célèbre celebrated legal case
caustic scathing (of speech)
cauterize to sear
cavalier disdainful, nonchalant
caveat warning
caveat emptor buyer beware
cavil quibble
cavort frolic
cede transfer ownership, relinquish
celestial heavenly
celibate abstaining from sex
cenotaph empty tomb, monument
censorious condemning speech
censure condemn

ceramics pottery
cerebral pertaining to the brain
cessation a stopping
chafe abrade
chagrin embarrassment
chalice goblet
champion defend
chaperon escort
charade pantomime, sham
charlatan quack, imposter
chartreuse greenish yellow
chary cautious
chaste pure, virgin
chasten castigate
chateau castle
cheeky brass, forward
cherub cupid
cherubic sweet, innocent
chicanery trickery
chide scold
chimerical imaginary, dreamlike

choleric easily angered
chortle laugh, snort
chronic continual (usually of illness)
chronicle a history, record
chronology arrangement by time
churl a boor
chutzpah gall
Cimmerian dim, unlit
cipher zero, nobody, a code
circa about (of time)
circuitous roundabout
circumcise remove the foreskin
circumlocution roundabout expression
circumspect cautious
circumvent evade, thwart
citadel fortress
citation summons to appear in court
clamor noise
clan extended family
clandestine secret
claustrophobia fear of enclosed places
cleave split
cleft split
clemency forgiveness
clique a small group
cloister refuge, monastery
clone duplicate
clout influence

cloven split
cloy glut, to sicken by excess
cloyed jaded
co-opt preempt, usurp
coagulate thicken
coalesce combine
coda concluding passage
coddle pamper
codicil supplement to a will
coercion force
coffer strongbox
cogent well-put, convincing
cogitate ponder
cognate from the same source
cognizant aware, mindful
cognomen family name
cohabit live together
cohere stick together
cohort an associate
coiffure hairdo
collaborate work together
collar seize, arrest
collateral securities for a debt
colloquial informal speech
colloquy conference
collusion conspiracy
colonnade row of columns

Quiz 6 (Antonyms)

<u>Directions:</u> Choose the word most opposite in meaning to the capitalized word. Answers are on page 101.

1. DERISION: (A) urgency (B) admonishment (C) uniqueness (D) diversity (E) acclaim

2. ANTIPATHY: (A) fondness (B) disagreement (C) boorishness (D) provocation (E) opprobrium

3. CAJOLE: (A) implore (B) glance at (C) belittle (D) ennoble (E) engender

4. CENSURE: (A) prevaricate (B) titillate (C) aggrandize (D) obscure (E) sanction

5. ADULATION: (A) immutability (B) reluctance (C) reflection (D) defamation (E) indifference

6. NOISOME: (A) salubrious (B) affable (C) multifarious (D) provident (E) officious

7. CONSECRATE: (A) curb (B) destroy (C) curse (D) inveigh (E) exculpate

8. ILLUSTRIOUS: (A) bellicose (B) ignoble (C) theoretical (D) esoteric (E) immaculate

9. DEIGN: (A) inveigh (B) gainsay (C) speculate (D) reject (E) laud

10. SUBTERFUGE: (A) bewilderment (B) artlessness (C) deceit (D) felicitation (E) jeopardy

comatose stupor
combine unite, blend
commandeer seize for military use
commemorate observe
commend praise
commensurate proportionate
commiserate empathize
commissary food store
commission authorization to perform a task
commodious spacious
commodity product
commodore naval officer
communion fellowship
commutation exchange, substitution
commute lessen punishment

compact covenant

compassion kindness

compatible well-matched, harmonious

compatriot countryman

compelling convincing, persuasive

compendium summary

compensate make up for

compensatory redeeming

competence skillfulness

compile collect

complacent self-satisfied, oblivious to coming danger

compliant submissive, conforming

complicity guilt by association

comport to conduct oneself

composed cool, self-possessed

compound augment

comprehensive thorough

comprise consist of

compulsive obsessive

compulsory obligatory

compunction remorse

concatenate link

concave curving inward

concede yield, grant

concerted done together, intensive effort

conch spiral shell

conciliatory reconciling, restoring goodwill

concise brief

conclusive convincing, ending doubt

concoct devise

concomitant accompanying, concurrent

concord accord

concordat agreement

concourse throng, open space for a gathering

concubine mistress

concur agree

concurrent simultaneous

condescend patronize, talk down to

condiment seasoning

condolence commiseration

condone overlook wrong doing, pardon

conducive helping

conduit pipe

confabulate discuss, give a fictitious account of a past event

confection candy

confederacy alliance

confer bestow

conference meeting

confidant trusted friend

confide trust another (with secrets)

confiscate seize

conflagration large fire

confluence flowing together

confound bewilder

confront challenge
confuse perplex
confute disprove
congeal solidify
congenial friendly
congenital inborn, existing from birth
congeries pile
congruence conformity
coniferous bearing cones
conjecture hypothesis, speculation
conjugal pertaining to marriage
conjure summon
connive conspire
connoisseur an expert, gourmet
consanguineous related by blood
conscientious honorable, upright
conscription draft, enlistment
consecrate make holy
consecutive one after another
consensus general agreement
considered well thought-out, contemplated
consign assign
consolation comfort, solace
console comfort
consolidate unite, strengthen
consonant harmonious
consort spouse
consortium cartel
conspicuous obvious

conspire plot
constellation arrangement of stars
consternation anxiety, bewilderment
constrained confined
construe interpret
consummate perfect
contagion infectious agent
contemplate meditate
contempt disdain
contend struggle
contented satisfied
contentious argumentative
contiguous adjacent, abutting
continence self-control
contingent conditional
contort twist
contraband illicit goods
contraction shrinkage
contractual related to a contract
contrariety opposition
contrast difference, comparison
contravene oppose
contretemps unfortunate occurrence
contrite apologetic
contrive arrange, artificial
controversial subject to dispute
controvert dispute
contumacy disobedience
contusion bruise

Quiz 7 (Matching)

Match each word in the first column with its definition in the second column. Answers are on page 101.

1. COMMANDEER
2. COMMUNION
3. COMPATRIOT
4. CONCERTED
5. CONCORD
6. CONFLUENCE
7. CONGERIES
8. CONSONANT
9. CONSUMMATE
10. CONTRITE

A. seize for military use
B. apologetic
C. perfect
D. accord
E. done together
F. pile
G. flowing together
H. harmonious
I. countryman
J. fellowship

conundrum puzzle, enigma

convene assemble (a group)

conventional customary, standard

converge come together

conversant familiar

converse opposite

convex curving outward

convey communicate

conviction strongly held belief

convivial sociable, festive

convocation gathering

convoke convene, summon

convoluted twisted, complicated

copious abundant

coquette a flirt

cordial friendly

cordon bond, chain, barrier

cornucopia cone-shaped horn filled with fruit

corollary consequence

coronation crowning of a sovereign

corporeal of the body

corps group of people

corpulent fat

corroborate confirm

cortege procession

coruscate sparkle

cosmopolitan worldly, sophisticated

cosset coddle

coterie small group

countenance facial expression

countermand overrule

counterstrike strike back

countervail counterbalance

coup masterstroke, sudden takeover

coup de grâce final stroke, a blow of mercy

court-martial military trial

courtesan prostitute

courtier member of the king's court

covenant agreement, pact

covert secret

covet desire
cower showing fear
crass crude
crave desire
craven cowardly
credence belief
credenza buffet
credulity gullibility
credulous believing
creed belief
crescendo becoming louder
crestfallen dejected
crevice crack
cringe cower
criterion a standard used in judging
critique examination, criticism
croon sing
cruet bottle
crux gist, key
cryptic mysterious, puzzling
cubism a style of painting
cudgel club
culinary pertaining to cooking
cull pick out, select
culminate climax
culpable blameworthy
culprit offender
culvert drain
cumbersome unwieldy

cumulative accumulate
cupidity greed
curb restrain, block
curmudgeon boor, bad-tempered
curriculum course of study
curry seek favor by flattery
cursory hasty
curt abrupt, rude
curtail shorten
cyclone storm
cynical scornful of the motives or sincerity of others
cynosure celebrity, center of attention
czar Russian emperor

D

dab touch lightly
dais platform
dally procrastinate, linger
dank cold and damp
dauntless courageous
de facto actual, in effect
de jure legally
de rigueur very formal, compulsory
deadpan expressionless
dearth scarcity
debacle a rout, defeat
debase degrade
debauch corrupt

Quiz 8 (Antonyms)

<u>Directions:</u> Choose the word most opposite in meaning to the capitalized word. Answers are on page 101.

1. UPSHOT: (A) consequence (B) descent (C) annihilation (D) termination (E) inception

2. WHET: (A) obscure (B) blunt (C) desiccate (D) imbibe (E) enervate

3. PRODIGY: (A) vacuous comment (B) hegemony (C) plane (D) common occurrence (E) capitulation

4. AMBULATORY: (A) immutable (B) obdurate (C) hospitalized (D) pedantic (E) stationary

5. PLATITUDE: (A) sincere comment (B) enigmatic comment (C) hostile comment (D) disingenuous comment (E) original comment

6. SEEMLY: (A) redoubtable (B) flaccid (C) imperceptible (D) indigenous (E) unbecoming

7. CHAMPION: (A) relinquish (B) contest (C) oppress (D) modify (E) withhold

8. AIR: (A) release (B) differ (C) expose (D) betray (E) enshroud

9. PERTURBATION: (A) impotence (B) obstruction (C) prediction (D) equanimity (E) chivalry

10: TEMPESTUOUS: (A) prodigal (B) reticent (C) serene (D) phenomenal (E) accountable

debauchery indulgence
debilitate weaken
debonair sophisticated, affable
debrief interrogate, inform
debunk refute, expose
debutante a girl debuting into society
decadence decay (e.g. moral or cultural)

decant pour
decapitate kill by beheading
decathlon athletic contest
deceive trick
deciduous shedding leaves
decimate destroy
decipher decode
decline decrease in number

decommission take a ship out of service

decorous seemly, dignified

decorum protocol, etiquette

decree official order

decrepitude enfeeblement

decry castigate

deduce conclude

deduct subtract

deem judge

deface mar, disfigure

defamation (noun) slander

defame (verb) slander

defeatist one who is resigned to defeat

defer postpone

deference courteously yielding to another

deficit shortage

defile pollute, corrupt

definitive conclusive, final

deflect turn aside

deflower despoil

defraud swindle

defray pay

deft skillful

defunct extinct

degrade demean

dehydrate dry out

deign condescend

deity a god

delectable delicious

delegate authorize

delete remove

deleterious harmful

deliberate ponder

delineate draw a line around, describe

delinquent negligent, culpable

delirium mental confusion, ecstasy

delude deceive

deluge a flood

delve dig, explore (of ideas)

demagogue a politician who appeals to base instincts

demean degrade

demeanor behavior

demented deranged

demise death

demobilize disband

demography study of human populations

demoralize dishearten

demote lower in rank

demur take (mild) exception, balk

demure sedate, reserved

denigrate defame

denizen dweller

denomination class, sect

denote signify, stand for

denouement resolution

denounce condemn
denude strip bare
depart leave
depict portray
deplete exhaust
deplore condemn
deploy arrange forces
deportment behavior, posture
deposition testimony
depravity immorality, wickedness
deprecate belittle
depredation preying on, plunder
deprive take away
deracinate uproot
derelict negligent
deride ridicule
derisive mocking
derogatory degrading
derrick crane
desecrate profane, defile
desiccate dehydrate
designate appoint
desist stop
desolate forsaken
despicable contemptible
despise loathe
despondent depressed
despot tyrant
destitute poor

desuetude disuse
desultory without direction in life
detached emotionally removed
detain confine
détente truce
detention confinement
deter discourage, prevent
deterrent hindrance, disincentive
detract lessen, undermine
detractor one who criticizes
detrimental harmful
detritus debris
devastate lay waste
deviate turn away from
devise plan
devoid empty
devotee enthusiast, follower
devout pious
diabolical devilish
dialectic pertaining to debate
diaphanous sheer, translucent
diatribe long denunciation
dicey risky
dichotomy a division into two parts
dictate command
dictum saying
didactic instructional
diffident shy
digress ramble

Quiz 9 (Matching)

Match each word in the first column with its definition in the second column. Answers are on page 101.

1. DEBUNK
2. DECIPHER
3. DEDUCE
4. DEFINITIVE
5. DEFUNCT
6. DELINEATE
7. DENOMINATION
8. DEPRECATE
9. DESOLATE
10. DIALECTIC

A. decode
B. refute
C. conclusive
D. conclude
E. to draw a line around
F. extinct
G. belittle
H. sect
I. pertaining to debate
J. forsaken

dilapidated neglected

dilate enlarge

dilatory procrastinating

dilemma a difficult choice

dilettante amateur, dabbler

diligent hard-working

diminution reduction

diocese district

dire dreadful

dirigible airship, blimp

disabuse correct

disaffect alienate

disarray disorder

disavow deny, disown

disband disperse

disburse pay out

discernible visible

discerning observant

disclaim renounce

disconcert confuse

disconsolate inconsolable

discord lack of harmony

discourse conversation

discreet prudent

discrepancy difference, disagreement

discrete separate

discretion prudence, the ability to make well-reasoned decisions

discriminating able to see differences

discursive rambling

disdain contempt

disengage release, detach

disfigure mar, ruin

disgruntled disappointed

dishevel muss

disinclination unwillingness

disingenuous deceptive, insincere

disinter unearth

disinterested impartial

disjointed disconnected, incoherent

dismal gloomy
dismantle take apart
dismay dread
disparage belittle
disparate various
disparity difference, inequality
dispassionate impartial
dispatch send
dispel cause to banish
disperse scatter
dispirit discourage
disposition attitude, temper
dispossess take away possessions
disputatious fond of arguing
dispute debate
disquietude anxiety
disquisition elaborate treatise
disrepute disgrace
dissemble pretend, hide true beliefs
disseminate distribute
dissent disagree with the majority
dissertation lecture
dissidence disagreement
dissipate scatter, squander
dissolute profligate, immoral
dissolution disintegration
dissonance discord
dissuade deter
distend swell

distortion misinterpret, lie
distract divert
distrait preoccupied, absent-minded
distraught distressed
distrust suspect
dither move without purpose
diurnal daily
diva prima donna
diverge branch off
diverse varying
diversion pastime
diversity variety
divest strip, deprive
dividend distributed profits
divine foretell
divisive causing conflict
divulge disclose
docile domesticated, trained
dock curtail
doctrinaire dogmatic
document verify
dodder tremble
dogged persistent
doggerel poor verse
dogmatic certain, unchanging in opinion
dolce sweetly and gently
doldrums dullness
doleful sorrowful

Quiz 10 (Antonyms)

<u>Directions:</u> Choose the word most opposite in meaning to the capitalized word. Answers are on page 101.

1. CURB: (A) bridle (B) encourage (C) reproach (D) ameliorate (E) perjure
2. DOCUMENT: (A) copy (B) implement (C) gainsay (D) blanch (E) rant
3. FLUID: (A) radiant (B) smooth (C) solid (D) balky (E) craggy
4. BOLT: (A) linger (B) refrain from (C) subdue (D) strip (E) transgress
5. TABLE: (A) palliate (B) acclimate (C) garner (D) propound (E) expedite
6. HARBOR: (A) provide shelter (B) banish (C) acquiesce (D) extol (E) capitulate
7. DISREPUTE: (A) impertinence (B) indifference (C) honor (D) affluence (E) apathy
8. STEEP: (A) desiccate (B) intensify (C) pontificate (D) whet (E) hamper
9. RENT: (A) reserved (B) restored (C) razed (D) busy (E) kinetic
10. EXACT: (A) extract (B) starve (C) lecture (D) menace (E) condone

dolorous gloomy
domicile home
dominion area of authority
don assume, put on
donor contributor
dormant asleep
dossier file
dotage senility
doting attending
double-entendre having two meanings one of which is sexually suggestive

doughty resolute, unafraid
dour sullen
dowager widow
doyen dean of a group
draconian harsh
dregs residue, riffraff
drivel inane speech
droll amusing
drone speak in a monotonic voice
dubious doubtful
ductile stretchable

dudgeon resentment, indignant humor
duenna governess
duet twosome
dulcet melodious
dupe one who is easily trick, victim
duplicity deceit, treachery
duress coercion
dynamic energetic

E

ebb recede
ebullient exuberant
eccentric odd, weird
ecclesiastical churchly
echelon degree, rank
éclat brilliance
eclectic from many sources
ectoderm top layer of skin
ecumenical universal, promoting unity
edict order
edifice building
edify instruct
editorialize express an opinion
educe draw forth, evoke
efface obliterate
effeminate unmanly
effervescence exuberance
effete worn out
efficacious effective
efficacy effectiveness
effigy likeness, mannequin
effloresce to bloom
effrontery insolence
effulgent brilliant
effusion pouring forth
egocentric self-centered
egregious grossly wrong
egress exit
ejaculate exclaim
eke supplement with great effort, strain
elaboration detailed explanation
elate raise spirits
electorate voters
eleemosynary pertaining to charity
elegant refined, exquisite
elegiac sad
elephantine large
elicit provoke
elide omit
elite upper-class
ellipsis omission of words
eloquent well-spoken
elucidate make clear, explain
elude evade
elusive evasive
emaciated underfed, gaunt
emancipate liberate

emasculate castrate, dispirit
embargo restriction
embellish exaggerate, adorn
embezzlement theft
emblazon imprint, brand
embody personify
embrace accept, adopt
embrangle embroil
embroil involve with trouble
embryonic rudimentary, nascent
emend correct
emergent appearing
emeritus retired, but retaining title
eminent distinguished, famous
emissary messenger
emote to display exaggerated emotion
empathy compassion, sympathy
employ make use of
empower enable, grant
emulate imitate
enact decree, ordain
enamored charmed, captivated
enate related on the mother's side
encapsulate condense
enchant charm
enclave area enclosed within another region
encomium praise
encompass contain, encircle

encore additional performance
encroach trespass
encumber burden
encyclopedic comprehensive
endear enamor
endeavor attempt, strive
endemic peculiar to a particular region
endocrinologist one who studies glands of internal secretion
endoderm within the skin
endorse approve
endowment property, gift
endure to suffer without giving up
enervate weaken
enfranchise liberate, grant the right to vote
engaging enchanting, charming
engender generate, prompt
engrave carve into a material
engross captivate
engulf overwhelm
enhance improve
enigmatic puzzling
enjoin urge, order, forbid
enlighten inform
enlist join
enmity hostility, hatred
ennoble exalt
ennui boredom, world-weariness

Quiz 11 (Matching)

Match each word in the first column with its definition in the second column. Answers are on page 101.

1. DORMANT
2. DOUGHTY
3. DUET
4. EBULLIENT
5. EFFEMINATE
6. ELLIPSIS
7. EMANCIPATE
8. ENCHANT
9. ENCYCLOPEDIC
10. ENIGMATIC

A. exuberant
B. puzzling
C. comprehensive
D. asleep
E. omission of words
F. unmanly
G. charm
H. liberate
I. twosome
J. resolute

enormity large, tragic

ensemble musical group

enshroud cover, obscure

ensnare trap, lure

ensue follow immediately

entail involve, necessitate

enterprise undertaking

enthrall mesmerize

entice lure

entomology the study of insects

entourage assemblage, staff

entreat plead

entrench fortify

entrepreneur businessman

enumerate count

enviable desirable

envision imagine, visualize

envoy messenger

eon long period of time

ephemeral short-lived

epic majestic, a long narrative poem

epicure gourmet

epidemic spreading rapidly

epidemiology study of the spread of disease

epigram saying

episode incident

epistemology the branch of philosophy dealing with knowledge

epithet name, appellation

epoch era

epoxy glue

equable even-tempered

equanimity composure, poise

equine pertaining to horses

equitable fair

equivocate make intentionally ambiguous

era period of time

eradicate abolish

ergo therefore

erode wear away
err mistake, misjudge
errant wandering
erratic constantly changing
erroneous mistaken
ersatz artificial
erudite learned
erupt burst forth
escalate intensify
escapade adventure
escarpment a steep slope
eschew avoid
esoteric known by only a few
esplanade boardwalk
espouse advocate
esteem respect
esthetic artistic
estimable meritorious
estrange alienate
eternal endless
ethereal light, airy
ethical conforming to accepted standards of behavior
ethos beliefs of a group
etiquette manners
etymology study of words
euphemism genteel expression
euphoria elation
euthanasia mercy-killing

evade avoid
evanescent fleeting, very brief
evangelical proselytizing
evasive elusive
eventful momentous
eventual ultimate, coming
eventuate bring about
evidential pertaining to evidence
evince attest, demonstrate
eviscerate disembowel
evoke draw forth
evolution gradual change
ewe female sheep
ex officio by virtue of position
exacerbate worsen
exact use authority to force payment
exacting demanding, difficult
exalt glorify
exasperate irritate
excerpt selection, extract
excision removal
exclaim shout
exclude shut out
exclusive prohibitive
excommunicate expel
excruciate torture
execrable abominable
execute put into effect
exegesis interpretation

Quiz 12 (Antonyms)

Directions: Choose the word most opposite in meaning to the capitalized word. Answers are on page 101.

1. DISCORD: (A) agreement   (B) supposition   (C) strife   (D) scrutiny   (E) antithesis

2. KEEN: (A) concentrated   (B) languid   (C) rash   (D) caustic   (E) voracious

3. IRRELEVANT: (A) moot   (B) onerous   (C) impertinent   (D) germane   (E) true

4. FACILITATE: (A) appease   (B) expedite   (C) extol   (D) foil   (E) precipitate

5. FEND: (A) absorb   (B) disperse   (C) intensify   (D) reflect   (E) halt

6. PORTLY: (A) ill   (B) thin   (C) dull   (D) rotund   (E) insipid

7. DEPLETE: (A) tax   (B) annotate   (C) replenish   (D) lecture   (E) vanquish

8. INCESSANT: (A) intermittent   (B) continual   (C) increasing   (D) enclosing   (E) expanding

9. PERJURE: (A) absolve   (B) forswear   (C) impeach   (D) authenticate   (E) mortify

10. PLETHORA: (A) dishonor   (B) paucity   (C) glut   (D) resolve   (E) deluge

exemplary outstanding

exempt excuse

exhaustive thorough

exhibitionist one who draws attention to himself

exhort strongly urge

exhume uncover

exigency urgency

exiguous scanty

exile banish

exodus departure, migration

exonerate free from blame

exorbitant expensive

exorcise expel

expanse extent of land

expansive sweeping

expedient advantageous
expedite hasten
expel drive out
expertise knowledge, ability
expiate atone
expletive curse, invective
expliate atone
explicate explain
explicit definite, clear
exploit utilize, milk
expose divulge, reveal
expostulate protest
expound explain
expropriate dispossess, confiscate
expunge erase
exquisite beautifully made
extant existing
extemporize improvise
extent scope
extenuate mitigate
extirpate seek out and destroy
extol praise highly
extort obtain under duress
extract to pull out, exact
extradite deport, deliver
extraneous not essential
extrapolate infer
extremity farthest point, boundary
extricate disentangle

extroverted outgoing
extrude force out
exuberant joyous
exude emit
exult rejoice

F

fabrication a lie
facade mask, front of a building
facet aspect
facetious joking, sarcastic
facile easy
facilitate make easier
facility skill
facsimile duplicate
faction clique, sect
factious causing disagreement
factitious artificial
factotum handyman
fallacious false
fallacy false belief
fallow unproductive, unplowed
falsetto high male voice
falter waver
fanaticism excessive zeal
fane temple
fanfare publicity
farcical absurd, ridiculous
farrago mixture

fascism totalitarianism, extreme nationalism

fastidious meticulous

fatal resulting in death

fathom understand

fatuity foolishness

fatuous inane, stupid

fauna animals

faux pas false step, mistake

fealty loyalty

feasible likely to succeed

feat deed, remarkable achievement

febrile feverish, delirious

feckless incompetent

fecund fertile

feign pretend

felicity happiness

felonious criminal

femme fatale a woman who leads men to their destruction

fend ward off

feral untamed, wild

ferment turmoil

ferret rummage through

fertile fruitful

fervor intensity

fester decay, to make someone increasingly bitter

festive joyous

festoon decorate

fete to honor with an event

fetid stinking

fetters shackles

fey eccentric, whimsical

fiasco debacle

fiat decree

fickle always changing one's mind

fictitious invented, imaginary

fidelity loyalty

figment falsehood, fantasy

filch steal

filial son

filibuster long speech

fillip stimulus

finale conclusion

finesse skill

firebrand agitator

firmament sky

fiscal monetary

fitful starting and stopping irregularly

fjord coastal inlet

flabbergasted amazed, dumbfounded

flagellate whip

flagrant outrageous, blatant

flail whip, to thrash something around uncontrollably and menacingly

fledgling just beginning, struggling

flippant pert, glib, dismissive

florid ruddy, ornate

Quiz 13 (Matching)

Match each word in the first column with its definition in the second column. Answers are on page 101.

1. EXHORT
2. EXONERATE
3. EXPOSTULATE
4. EXTRADITE
5. EXULT
6. FACTITIOUS
7. FATUOUS
8. FERAL
9. FIASCO
10. FIREBRAND

A. free from blame
B. strongly urge
C. agitator
D. untamed
E. debacle
F. inane
G. artificial
H. deport
I. rejoice
J. protest

flout to show disregard for the law or rules

fluctuate waver, vary

foible weakness, minor fault

foil defeat, thwart

foist palm off a fake

foment instigate

font source, fountainhead, set of type

forage search for food

foray raid

forbear abstain, restrain oneself

force majeure superior force

foreboding ominous

foreclose exclude

forensic pertaining to debate

foresight ability to predict the future

forestall thwart, preempt

forgo relinquish (usually voluntarily)

forsake abandon

forswear deny

forthright frank

forthwith immediately

fortify strengthen

fortitude resilience, courage

fortuitous lucky

foster encourage, cultivate

founder sink, fail

fracas noisy fight

fragile easily broken

fragmented broken into fragments

fraternity brotherhood

fraught filled

frenetic harried, neurotic

fret worry

fritter squander

frivolity playfulness

frolic romp, play

frond bending tree

frugal thrifty

fruitful productive

fruition realization, completion
fruitless unprofitable, barren
fulminate denounce, menace
fulsome excessive, insincere
fuming angry
furlough leave of absence
furor commotion
furtive stealthy
fusillade bombardment
futile hopeless

G

gaffe embarrassing mistake
gainful profitable
gainsay contradict
galvanize excite to action
gambit plot, strategy
gamut range, scope
gargantuan large
garner gather
garnish decorate
garrote stranglehold
garrulous talkative
gauche awkward
genealogy ancestry
generic general
genesis beginning
genetics study of heredity
genre kind, category
genteel elegant, refined
genuflect kneel in reverence
genuine authentic, sincere
geriatrics pertaining to old age
germane relevant
ghastly horrible
gibe heckle
gingivitis inflammation of the gums
gist essence (of an argument)
glabrous without hair
glaucoma disorder of the eye
glean gather
glib insincere manner
glower stare angrily
glut surplus, excess
glutton one who eats too much
gnarl deform
gnome dwarf-like being
goad encourage, provoke
googol a very large number
gorge stuff, satiate
gorgon ugly person
gormandize eat voraciously
gory bloody
gossamer thin and flimsy
Gothic medieval style of architecture
gouge overcharge
gracious kindness, politeness
gradient incline, rising by degrees

Quiz 14 (Antonyms)

<u>Directions:</u> Choose the word most opposite in meaning to the capitalized word. Answers are on page 101.

1. ASSIMILATE: (A) strive (B) adapt (C) synchronize (D) estrange (E) officiate

2. INADVERTENT: (A) accidental (B) disingenuous (C) forthright (D) inconsiderate (E) calculated

3. ABSCOND: (A) pilfer (B) replace (C) glean (D) substitute (E) surrender

4. FOMENT: (A) exhort (B) dissuade (C) cower (D) abet (E) fixate

5. EXTENUATE: (A) alleviate (B) preclude (C) worsen (D) subdue (E) justify

6. NONPAREIL: (A) consummate (B) juvenile (C) dutiful (D) ordinary (E) choice

7. REPUDIATE: (A) denounce (B) deceive (C) embrace (D) fib (E) generalize

8. NOXIOUS: (A) diffuse (B) latent (C) beneficial (D) unique (E) unjust

9. SUFFRAGE: (A) absence of charity (B) absence of franchise (C) absence of pain (D) absence of success (E) absence of malice

10. GLEAN: (A) gaffe (B) furor (C) gather (D) frolic (E) foist

gradual by degrees, changing slowly
grandiose impressive, large
granular grainy
grapple struggle
gratis free
gratitude thankfulness
gratuitous unwarranted, uncalled for
gratuity tip
gravamen the essential part of an accusation
gravity seriousness
gregarious sociable
grievous tragic, heinous
grimace expression of disgust or pain
grisly gruesome
grovel crawl, obey, beg

grudging reluctant
guffaw laughter
guile deceit
gullible easily deceived
gusto great enjoyment
guttural throaty
gyrate whirl

H

habitat natural environment
habituate accustom
hackneyed trite
haggard gaunt
halcyon serene
hale healthy
hallucination delusion
hamper obstruct
hapless unlucky
harangue tirade
harass torment
harbinger forerunner
harbor give shelter, conceal
hardy healthy
harlequin clown
harp complain incessantly
harridan hag
harrowing distressing
harry harass
haughty arrogant

haven refuge
havoc destruction, chaos
hearsay gossip
hedonism the pursuit of pleasure in life
heed follow advice
heedless careless
hegemony authority, domination
hegira a journey to a more pleasant place
heinous vile, atrocious
heliocentric having the sun as a center
helix a spiral
helots slaves
herald harbinger
herbivorous feeding on plants
Herculean powerful, large
hermetic airtight, sealed
hermit one who lives in solitude
herpetologist one who studies reptiles
heterodox departing form established doctrines
heuristic teaching device or method
hew cut
heyday glory days, prime
hiatus interruption
hibernal wintry
hidalgo nobleman
hidebound prejudiced, provincial

hideous horrible
hie to hasten
highbrow intellectual
hirsute bearded
histrionic overly dramatic
holograph written entirely by hand
homage respect
homely plain
homily sermon
homogeneous uniform
homonym words that are identical in spelling and pronunciation
hone sharpen
horde group
hortatory inspiring good deeds
hospice shelter
hovel shanty, cabin
hoyden tomboy
hubris arrogance
hue color
humane compassionate
humanities languages and literature
humility humbleness
hummock knoll, mound
humus soil
husbandry management
hybrid crossbreed
hydrophobia fear of water
hygienic sanitary

hymeneal pertaining to marriage
hymn religious song
hyperactive overactive
hyperbole exaggeration
hypertension elevated blood pressure
hypocritical deceiving, two-faced
hypoglycemic low blood sugar
hypothermia low body temperature

I

ibidem in the same place
ichthyology study of fish
iconoclast one who rails against sacred institutions
idiosyncrasy peculiarity
idyllic natural, picturesque
ignoble dishonorable
ilk class, clan
illicit unlawful
illimitable limitless
illusory fleeting, deceptive
illustrious famous
imbibe drink
imbue infuse
immaculate spotlessly clean
immaterial irrelevant
immense huge

Quiz 15 (Matching)

Match each word in the first column with its definition in the second column. Answers are on page 101.

1. GRANDIOSE
2. GRIEVOUS
3. HALCYON
4. HARLEQUIN
5. HEDONISM
6. HEURISTIC
7. HIDEBOUND
8. HUBRIS
9. HYMENEAL
10. IMBIBE

A. drink
B. pertaining to marriage
C. arrogance
D. prejudiced
E. teaching device or method
F. the pursuit of pleasure in life
G. clown
H. serene
I. heinous
J. impressive

immerse bathe, engross

imminent about to happen

immobile still

immolate sacrifice (especially by fire)

immunity exemption from prosecution

immure build a wall around

immutable unchangeable, absolute

impair injure

impale pierce

impartial not biased

impasse deadlock

impassioned fiery, emotional

impassive calm

impeach accuse, charge

impeccable faultless

impecunious indigent

impede hinder

impediment obstacle

impel urge, force

impending approaching, imminent

imperative vital, pressing

imperceptible slight, intangible

imperialism colonialism

imperil endanger

imperious domineering

impertinent insolent

imperturbable calm, unflappable

impervious impenetrable, unreceptive

impetuous impulsive

impetus stimulus, spark

impinge encroach, touch

implant instill

implausible unlikely, improbable

implement carry out, execute

implicate incriminate

implicit implied

implore entreat

implosion bursting inward

impolitic unwise, inappropriate

45

imponderable difficult to estimate

import meaning, significance

importune urgent request

imposing intimidating, stately

imposition intrusion, burden

impotent powerless

impound seize

imprecation curse, inculcate

impregnable invincible

impresario promoter

impressionable susceptible, easily influenced

impressionism a style of painting

imprimatur sanction

impromptu spontaneous

improvise invent

impudence insolence

impugn criticize, accuse

impulse inclination, sudden desire

impulsive to act suddenly

impunity exemption from harm

impute charge

in toto in full, entirely

inadvertent unintentional

inadvisable not recommended

inalienable that which cannot be taken away

inane vacuous, stupid

inanimate inorganic, lifeless

inaudible cannot be heard

inaugurate induct (with a ceremony)

inborn innate

incalculable immeasurable

incandescent brilliant

incantation chant

incapacitate disable

incarcerate imprison

incarnate embody, personify

incendiary inflammatory

incense enrage

incentive stimulus, inducement

incessant unceasing

incest sex among family members

inchoate just begun

incidental insignificant, minor

incinerate burn

incipient beginning

incision cut

incisive keen, penetrating

incite foment, provoke

incivility rudeness

inclement harsh, stormy

inclusive comprehensive

incognito disguised

incommunicado unable to communicate with others

incomparable peerless

incompatibility inability to live in harmony

Quiz 16 (Analogies)

Directions: Choose the pair that expresses a relationship most similar to that expressed in the capitalized pair. Answers are on page 101.

1. ANARCHY : GOVERNMENT ::
   - (A) confederation : state
   - (B) trepidation : courage
   - (C) serenity : equanimity
   - (D) surfeit : food
   - (E) computer : hard drive

2. Galvanize : Charismatic Leader ::
   - (A) jeer : fan
   - (B) correct : charlatan
   - (C) impeach : President
   - (D) retreat : champion
   - (E) moderate : arbiter

3. PARRY : BLOW ::
   - (A) equivocate : question
   - (B) cower : start
   - (C) boomerang : backlash
   - (D) cast : invective
   - (E) browbeat : chastity

4. DISQUIETUDE : ANXIOUS ::
   - (A) magnitude : unabridged
   - (B) isolation : sequestered
   - (C) cupidity : bellicose
   - (D) embellishment : overstated
   - (E) nonplus : perplexed

5. MILK : DRAIN ::
   - (A) insult : commend
   - (B) abstract : distend
   - (C) extend : disregard
   - (D) exploit : employ
   - (E) assail : rescind

6. ABSTRUSE : CLEAR ::
   - (A) nondescript : conspicuous
   - (B) high-brow : indifferent
   - (C) affable : agreeable
   - (D) prominent : manifest
   - (E) complex : hard

7. OMNISCIENT : KNOWLEDGE ::
   - (A) saturnine : energy
   - (B) complete : retraction
   - (C) principled : method
   - (D) inquisitive : science
   - (E) boundless : expanse

8. STOKE : SMOTHER ::
   - (A) incinerate : heat
   - (B) animate : enervate
   - (C) contest : decry
   - (D) acknowledge : apprehend
   - (E) garrote : asphyxiate

9. ORCHESTRA : MUSICIAN ::
   - (A) story : comedian
   - (B) band : singer
   - (C) garden : leaf
   - (D) troupe : actor
   - (E) government : lawyer

10. MUTTER : INDISTINCT ::
    - (A) define : easy
    - (B) blunder : polished
    - (C) articulate : well-spoken
    - (D) expedite : completed
    - (E) censure : histrionic

inconceivable unthinkable

incongruous out of place, absurd

inconsiderate thoughtless, insensitive

inconspicuous not noticeable

incontrovertible indisputable

incorporate combine

incorrigible unreformable
incredulous skeptical
increment step, increase
incriminate accuse
incubus nightmare
inculcate instill, indoctrinate
inculpate accuse
incumbent obligatory
incursion raid
indecent offensive, lewd
indecorous unseemly
indelible permanent
indemnity insurance
indict charge
indifferent unconcerned
indigenous native
indigent poor
indignant resentment of injustice
indiscreet lacking sound judgment, rash
indiscriminate random
indispensable vital, essential
indistinct blurry, without clear features
indolent lazy
indomitable invincible
indubitable unquestionable
induce persuade, provoke
indulge succumb to desire
indurate harden

industrious hard-working
inebriate intoxicate
ineffable inexpressible
ineffectual futile
ineluctable inescapable
inept unfit, incompetent
inert inactive
inestimable priceless, immeasurable
inevitable unavoidable, predestined
inexorable relentless
infallible unerring
infamous notorious
infamy shame
infantry foot soldiers
infatuate immature love
infer conclude
infernal hellish
infidel nonbeliever
infidelity disloyalty
infiltrate trespass
infinitesimal very small
infirmary clinic
infirmity ailment
inflammatory incendiary
influx inflow
infraction violation
infringe encroach
infuriate enrage
infuse inspire, instill

ingenious clever, resourceful

ingrate ungrateful person

ingratiate pleasing, flattering, endearing

ingress entering

inherent innate, inborn

inhibit restrain

inimical adverse, hostile

inimitable peerless

iniquitous unjust, wicked

iniquity sin, injustice

initiate begin

initiation induction ceremony

injunction command

inkling hint

innate inborn

innervate invigorate

innocuous harmless

innovative new, useful idea

innuendo insinuation

inopportune untimely

inordinate excessive

inquest investigation

inquisition interrogation

inquisitive curious

insatiable gluttonous

inscribe engrave

inscrutable cannot be fully understood

insensate without feeling

insidious treacherous, sinister

insignia emblems

insinuate allude

insipid flat, dull

insolent insulting

insolvent bankrupt

insouciant nonchalant

installment portion, payment

instant at once

instigate incite

insubordinate disobedient

insufferable unbearable

insular narrow-minded

insuperable insurmountable

insurgent rebellious

insurrection uprising

intangible not perceptible by touch

integral essential

integrate make whole

integration unification

integument a covering

intelligentsia the intellectual elite of society

intensive extreme, concentrated

inter bury

intercede plead on behalf of another

intercept prevent, cut off

interdict prohibit

interject interrupt

Quiz 17 (Matching)

Match each word in the first column with its definition in the second column. Answers are on page 101.

1. INCONGRUOUS
2. INCONSPICUOUS
3. INDECOROUS
4. INDIGNANT
5. INDURATE
6. INEXORABLE
7. INIMICAL
8. INSCRUTABLE
9. INSOUCIANT
10. INSUPERABLE

A. harden
B. relentless
C. hostile
D. cannot be fully understood
E. out of place, absurd
F. not noticeable
G. unseemly
H. resentment of injustice
I. nonchalant
J. insurmountable

interloper intruder

interlude intermission

interminable unending

internecine mutually destructive

interpolate insert

interpose insert

interregnum interval between two successive reigns

interrogate question

intersperse scatter

interstate between states

intervene interfere, mediate

intestate leaving no will

intimate allude to, hint

intractable unmanageable

intransigent unyielding

intrepid fearless

intricate complex

intrigue plot, mystery

intrinsic inherent

introspection self-analysis

inundate flood

inure accustom, habituate, harden

invalidate disprove, nullify

invective verbal insult

inveigh to rail against

inveigle lure, wheedle

inventive cleaver, resourceful

inverse directly opposite

inveterate habitual, chronic

invidious incurring ill-will

invincible cannot be defeated

inviolate sacred, unchangeable

invocation calling on God

irascible irritable

irate angry

ironic oddly contrary to what is expected

irrational illogical

irrelevant unrelated, immaterial

irreparable cannot be repaired

irresolute hesitant, uncertain

irrevocable cannot be rescinded
isosceles having two equal sides
itinerant wandering
itinerary route

J

jabberwocky nonsense
jaded spent, bored with one's situation
jargon specialized vocabulary
jaundiced biased, embittered
jeer mock
jejune barren, unsophisticated
jest joke
jilt reject, end a relationship promptly
jingoistic nationalistic, warmongering
jocular humorous
jostle push, brush against
journeyman reliable worker
joust combat between knights on horses
jubilant in high spirits
judicious prudent
juggernaut unstoppable force
jugular throat
juncture pivotal point in time
junoesque stately beauty
junta small ruling group
jurisdiction domain
jurisprudence law
justify excuse, mitigate
juvenescent making young, growing out of infancy and into childhood
juxtapose to place side by side

K

kaleidoscope series of changing events
keen of sharp mind
ken purview, range of comprehension
kindle arouse, inspire
kindred similar, related by blood
kinetic pertaining to motion
kismet fate, the will of Allah
kite bad check
kitsch trashy art
kleptomania impulse to steal
knave con man
knead massage, to fold, press, and stretch a substance into a uniform mass
knell sound of a bell
Koran holy book of Islam
kowtow behave obsequiously
kudos acclaim

L

labyrinth maze
lacerate tear, cut

Quiz 18 (Analogies)

Directions: Choose the pair that expresses a relationship most similar to that expressed in the capitalized pair. Answers are on page 101.

1. LOQUACIOUS : GARRULOUS ::
    - (A) harsh : kindly
    - (B) animate : weary
    - (C) gluttonous : disloyal
    - (D) rash : impetuous
    - (E) blithe : gloomy

2. EMPATHY : FEELING ::
    - (A) melancholy : joy
    - (B) sibling : relative
    - (C) Spartan : wickedness
    - (D) boldness : guilt
    - (E) institution : encouragement

3. DEVIATE : LECTURE ::
    - (A) broadcast : information
    - (B) disown : friend
    - (C) welcome : indifference
    - (D) entreat : solicitation
    - (E) meander : drive

4. NEBULOUS : FORM ::
    - (A) insincere : misanthrope
    - (B) benevolent : excellence
    - (C) insipid : taste
    - (D) discerning : hope
    - (E) composed : innocence

5. PENSIVE : MELANCHOLY ::
    - (A) scornful : contempt
    - (B) confident : victory
    - (C) eloquent : optimism
    - (D) sorrowful : indifference
    - (E) contumacious : esteem

6. ANATHEMA : CURSE ::
    - (A) hex : blessing
    - (B) admonition : censure
    - (C) incantation : discernment
    - (D) theory : calculation
    - (E) conjecture : truth

7. DILIGENT : ASSIDUOUS ::
    - (A) suspicious : reliable
    - (B) cautious : indecisive
    - (C) repentant : innocent
    - (D) peerless : common
    - (E) indigent : poor

8. LAMPOON : MOCK ::
    - (A) exalt : ennoble
    - (B) entice : disown
    - (C) prattle : talk
    - (D) entreat : controvert
    - (E) debate : heckle

9. INTUITIVE : CONSIDERED ::
    - (A) impromptu : planning
    - (B) laborious : safe
    - (C) ethereal : light
    - (D) random : sequential
    - (E) rational : certain

10. ETERNAL : EPHEMERAL ::
    - (A) equivocal : ambiguous
    - (B) hopeless : chance
    - (C) animated : blithe
    - (D) mysterious : perplexing
    - (E) foreign : familiar

lachrymose tearful
lackey servant
laconic brief, terse
lactic derived from milk
lacuna a missing part, gap
laggard loafer, slacker

lagniappe bonus
laity laymen
lambent softly radiant
lament mourn
lamina layer
lampoon satirize
languish weaken
lanyard short rope
larceny theft
largess generous donation
lascivious lustful
lassitude lethargy
latent potential, dormant
laudatory commendable
laurels fame, success
lave wash
lavish extravagant
lax loose, careless
laxity carelessness
layman nonprofessional
lectern reading desk
leery cautious, doubtful
legacy bequest
legerdemain trickery
legible readable
legislate make laws
legitimate lawful
lenient forgiving
lethargic drowsy, sluggish
levee embankment, dam
leviathan a monster
levity frivolity
liable legally responsible
liaison relationship, affair
libertarian one who believes in complete freedom
libertine roué, rake
libidinous lustful
licentious lewd, immoral
lien financial claim
lieutenant one who acts in place of another
ligature bond
ligneous wood like
Lilliputian very small
limerick poem
limn portray, describe
limpid transparent, clearly understood
linchpin something that is indispensable
lineage ancestry
linguistics study of language
liquidate eliminate
lissome agile, supple
listless lacking spirit or interest
litany list
lithe supple
litigate contest with a lawsuit

litotes two negative statement that cancel to make a positive statement

liturgy ceremony

livid enraged

loath reluctant

loathe abhor, dislike

lofty high

logistics means of supplying troops

logo symbol

logy sluggish

loquacious talkative

lothario rake, womanizer

lout goon, hoodlum

lucid clearly understood

lucrative profitable

lucre money, profit

ludicrous absurd

lugubrious extremely sad

luminous bright

lupine wolf-like

lure entice

lurid ghastly, sensational

luster gloss, sheen

luxuriant lush, lavish

lynch to execute by hanging without a trial

M

macabre gruesome

Machiavellian politically crafty, cunning

machination plot

macrobiosis longevity

macroscopic visibly large

maelstrom whirlpool

magisterial arbitrary, dictatorial

magnanimous generous, kindhearted

magnate a powerful, successful person (especially of business)

magnitude size

magnum opus masterpiece

maim injure, disfigure

maladjusted disturbed

maladroit clumsy

malady illness

malaise uneasiness, weariness

malapropism comical misuse of a word

malcontent one who is forever dissatisfied

malediction curse

malefactor evildoer

malevolence bad intent, malice

malfeasance wrong doing (especially by an official of government)

malice spite

malign defame

malignant virulent, pernicious

malinger shirk

malleable moldable, tractable

Quiz 19 (Matching)

Match each word in the first column with its definition in the second column. Answers are on page 101.

1. LACHRYMOSE
2. LAGGARD
3. LASCIVIOUS
4. LEGERDEMAIN
5. LIBERTINE
6. LILLIPUTIAN
7. LOQUACIOUS
8. MACHIAVELLIAN
9. MAGISTERIAL
10. MALAPROPISM

A. trickery
B. roué
C. very small
D. tearful
E. loafer
F. lustful
G. talkative
H. comical misuse of a word
I. arbitrary, dictatorial
J. politically crafty, cunning

malodorous fetid

mammoth huge

manacle shackle

mandate command

mandatory obligatory

mandrill baboon

mania madness, obsession

manifest obvious, evident

manifesto proclamation

manifold multiple, diverse

manslaughter killing another person without malice

manumit set free

manuscript unpublished book

mar damage

marauder plunderer

marginal insignificant

marionette puppet

maroon abandon

marshal array, mobilize

martial warlike

martinet disciplinarian

martyr sacrifice, symbol

masochist one who enjoys pain

masticate chew

mastiff large dog

mastodon extinct elephant

maternal motherly

maternity motherhood

matriarch matron

matriculate enroll (usually in school)

matrix array

matutinal early, morning

maudlin weepy, sentimental

maul rough up

mausoleum tomb

maverick a rebel, individualist

mawkish sickeningly sentimental

mayhem mutilation, chaos

mea culpa my fault

meager scanty
meander roam, ramble
median middle
mediocre average
medley mixture
megalith ancient stone monument
melancholy reflective, gloomy
melee riot
mellifluous sweet sounding
melodious melodic
memento souvenir
memoir autobiography
memorabilia things worth remembering
memorandum note
menagerie zoo
mendacity untruth
mendicant beggar
menial humble, degrading
mentor teacher
mercantile commercial
mercenary calculating, venal
mercurial changeable, volatile
metamorphosis a change in form
mete distribute
meteoric swift, dazzling
meteorology science of weather
methodical systematic, careful
meticulous extremely careful, precise

metier occupation
metonymy the substitution of a phrase for the name itself
mettle courage, capacity for bravery
miasma toxin fumes
mien appearance, bearing
migrate travel
milieu environment
militant combative, activist
militate work against
milk extract
millennium thousand-year period
minatory threatening
mince chop, moderate
minion subordinate
minstrel troubadour
minuscule small
minute very small
minutiae trivia
mirage illusion
mire marsh, a situation that is difficult to escape from
mirth jollity
misanthrope hater of mankind
misappropriation use dishonestly
misbegotten illegitimate, obtained by dishonest means
miscarry abort
miscegenation intermarriage between races

Quiz 20 (Analogies)

Directions: Choose the pair that expresses a relationship most similar to that expressed in the capitalized pair. Answers are on page 101.

1. SPEECH : FILIBUSTER ::
   - (A) race : marathon
   - (B) gift : breach
   - (C) statement : digression
   - (D) detour : path
   - (E) address : postage

2. ARISTOCRAT : LAND ::
   - (A) bureaucracy : enslavement
   - (B) monarchy : abnegation
   - (C) gentry : talent
   - (D) dignitary : rank
   - (E) junta : anarchy

3. SURREPTITIOUS : STEALTH ::
   - (A) clandestine : openness
   - (B) guarded : effrontery
   - (C) bombastic : irreverence
   - (D) pernicious : bane
   - (E) impertinent : humility

4. PECCADILLO : FLAW ::
   - (A) mediator : dispute
   - (B) grammar : error
   - (C) nick : score
   - (D) forensics : judiciary
   - (E) invasion : putsch

5. LEVEE : RIVER ::
   - (A) rampart : barrier
   - (B) cordon : throng
   - (C) broker : investment
   - (D) promontory : height
   - (E) string : guitar

6. HEDONIST : UNSTINTING ::
   - (A) protagonist : insignificant
   - (B) thug : aggressive
   - (C) politician : irresolute
   - (D) benefactor : generous
   - (E) drunkard : manifest

7. EXCERPT : NOVEL ::
   - (A) critique : play
   - (B) review : manuscript
   - (C) swatch : cloth
   - (D) foreword : preface
   - (E) recital : performance

8. EXORCISM : DEMON ::
   - (A) matriculation : induction
   - (B) banishment : member
   - (C) qualm : angel
   - (D) heuristic : method
   - (E) manifesto : spirit

9. HOPE : CYNICAL ::
   - (A) reticence : benevolent
   - (B) contention : bellicose
   - (C) bliss : sullen
   - (D) homage : industrious
   - (E) unconcern : indifferent

10. Exhibitionist : Attention ::
    - (A) sycophant : turmoil
    - (B) scientist : power
    - (C) megalomaniac : solitude
    - (D) martyr : anonymity
    - (E) mercenary : money

miscellany mixture of items
misconstrue misinterpret
miscreant evildoer

misgiving doubt, hesitation
misnomer wrongly named
misogyny hatred of women

misshapen deformed
missive letter
mitigate lessen the severity
mnemonics that which aids the memory
mobilize assemble for action
mobocracy rule by mob
modicum pittance
modish chic
module unit
mogul powerful person
molest bother, sexually assault
mollify appease
molten melted
momentous of great importance
monocle eyeglass
monolithic large and uniform
monologue long speech
monstrosity distorted, abnormal form
moot disputable, no longer relevant
moral ethical
morale spirit, confidence
morass swamp, difficult situation
moratorium postponement
mordant biting, sarcastic
mores moral standards
moribund near death
morose sullen
morphine painkilling drug
morsel bite, piece

mortify humiliate
mosque temple
mote speck
motif artistic theme
motive reason for doing something
motley diverse
mottled spotted
motto slogan, saying
mountebank charlatan
mousy drab, colorless
muckraker reformer
muffle stifle, quiet
mulct defraud
multifarious diverse, many-sided
multitude throng
mundane ordinary
munificent generous
murmur mutter, mumble
muse ponder
muster to gather one's forces
mutability able to change
mute silent
mutilate maim
mutiny rebellion
mutter murmur, grumble
muzzle restrain, stifle
myopic narrow-minded
myriad innumerable
myrmidons loyal followers

mystique mystery, aura
mythical fictitious

N

nadir lowest point
narcissism self-love
narrate tell, recount
nascent incipient
natal related to birth
nativity the process of birth
naturalize grant citizenship
ne'er-do-well loafer, idler
nebulous indistinct
necromancy sorcery
nefarious evil
negate cancel
negligible insignificant
nemesis implacable foe
neologism newly coined expression
neonatal newborn
neophyte beginner
nepotism favoritism
nervy brash
nether under
nettle irritate
neurotic disturbed
neutralize offset, nullify
nexus a link between two or more people or things

nicety euphemism
niche nook, an activity that well suits a person's talents
niggardly stingy
nimble spry
nirvana bliss, the attainment of spiritual enlightenment
noctambulism sleepwalking
nocturnal pertaining to night
nocturne serenade
noisome harmful, disgusting
nomad wanderer
nomenclature terminology
nominal slight, in name only
nominate propose, recommend somebody for a position
nominee candidate
nonchalant casual
noncommittal neutral, circumspect
nondescript lacking distinctive features
nonentity person of no significance
nonesuch paragon, one in a thousand
nonpareil unequaled, peerless
nonpartisan neutral, uncommitted
nonplus confound, befuddle
notable remarkable, noteworthy
noted famous
notorious wicked, widely known
nouveau riche newly rich

Quiz 21 (Matching)

Match each word in the first column with its definition in the second column. Answers are on page 101.

1. MISCELLANY
2. MISSIVE
3. MOOT
4. MOUNTEBANK
5. MULTIFARIOUS
6. MUSTER
7. MYRMIDONS
8. NARCISSISM
9. NEOLOGISM
10. NONPAREIL

A. peerless
B. to gather one's forces
C. newly coined expression
D. self-love
E. loyal followers
F. letter
G. diverse
H. charlatan
I. disputable
J. mixture of items

nova bright star

novel new, unique

novice beginner

noxious toxic

nuance shade, subtlety

nub crux, crucial point

nubile marriageable

nugatory useless, worthless

nuisance annoyance

nullify void

nullity nothingness

numismatics coin collecting

nurture nourish, foster

nymph goddess

O

oaf awkward person

obdurate unyielding, hardhearted

obeisance homage, deference

obelisk tall column, monument

obese fat

obfuscate bewilder, muddle

obituary eulogy

objective (adj.) unbiased

objective (noun) goal

objectivity impartiality

oblation offering, sacrifice

obligatory required, compulsory

oblige compel

obliging accommodating, considerate

oblique indirect

obliquity perversity

obliterate destroy

oblong elliptical, oval

obloquy slander

obscure vague, unclear

obsequious fawning, servile

obsequy funeral ceremony

observant watchful

obsolete outdated

obstinate stubborn

obstreperous noisy, unruly

obtain gain possession

obtrusive forward, meddlesome

obtuse stupid

obviate make unnecessary

Occident the West

occlude block

occult mystical, secret, relating to the supernatural or witchcraft

octogenarian person in her eighties

ocular optic, visual

ode poem

odious despicable

odoriferous pleasant odor

odyssey journey

offal inedible parts of a butchered animal

offertory church collection

officiate supervise

officious forward, obtrusive

offset counterbalance

ogle flirt

ogre monster, demon

oleaginous oily

oligarchy aristocracy

olio medley

ominous threatening

omnibus collection, compilation

omnipotent all-powerful

omniscient all-knowing

onerous burdensome

onslaught powerful attack

ontology the study of the nature of existence

onus burden

opaque nontransparent

operative working

operetta musical comedy

opiate narcotic

opine think, express an opinion

opportune well-timed, appropriate

oppress persecute

oppressive burdensome

opprobrious abusive, scornful

opprobrium disgrace

oppugn assail

opt decide, choose

optimum best condition

optional elective

opulence wealth

opus literary work or musical composition

oracle prophet

oration speech

orator speaker

orb sphere

orchestrate organize

ordain appoint

Quiz 22 (Analogies)

Directions: Choose the pair that expresses a relationship most similar to that expressed in the capitalized pair. Answers are on page 101.

1. PARAGRAPH : ESSAY ::
   - (A) trailer : automobile
   - (B) query : question
   - (C) instrument : surgery
   - (D) penmanship : essay
   - (E) shot : salvo

2. COMPOUND : BUILDING ::
   - (A) classroom : campus
   - (B) department : government
   - (C) tapestry : fabric
   - (D) seed : vegetable
   - (E) commonwealth : country

3. CONSTELLATION : STARS ::
   - (A) amplifier : hearing
   - (B) ocean : water
   - (C) mosaic : tile
   - (D) tracks : train
   - (E) book : paper

4. ACCELERATE : VELOCITY ::
   - (A) relinquish : assets
   - (B) energize : stamina
   - (C) protect : parent
   - (D) project : futility
   - (E) educate : stupor

5. SIDEREAL : STARS ::
   - (A) platonic : radiation
   - (B) avian : fish
   - (C) corporeal : heaven
   - (D) heliocentric : transportation
   - (E) terrestrial : Earth

6. STATE : CONFEDERACY ::
   - (A) apple : tree
   - (B) return address : envelope
   - (C) binoculars : sight
   - (D) velocity : acceleration
   - (E) soldier : army

7. HELPFUL : OFFICIOUS ::
   - (A) difficult : incorrigible
   - (B) maudlin : sardonic
   - (C) apathetic : zealous
   - (D) true : contrary
   - (E) friendly : amiable

8. SATURATE : DAMPEN ::
   - (A) contaminate : pollute
   - (B) besmirch : sully
   - (C) extol : praise
   - (D) waive : donate
   - (E) pronounce : presume

9. WAYLAY : ADVANCEMENT ::
   - (A) corroborate : testimony
   - (B) amuse : jeopardy
   - (C) condescend : frenzy
   - (D) curb : movement
   - (E) negotiate : defeat

10. MITIGATE : INJURY ::
    - (A) exacerbate : recovery
    - (B) palliate : accusation
    - (C) dampen : enthusiasm
    - (D) darken : obscurity
    - (E) entreat : ultimatum

orderly neat, arranged
ordinance law
ordnance artillery
orient align, familiarize
orison prayer
ornate lavishly decorated

ornithology study of birds
orthodox conventional
oscillate waver, swing
ossify harden
ostensible apparent, seeming
ostentatious pretentious
ostracize banish, shun
otherworldly spiritual
otiose idle
ouster ejection
outmoded out-of-date
outré eccentric
outset beginning
ovation applause
overrule disallow
overture advance, proposal
overweening arrogant, forward
overwhelm overpower
overwrought overworked, high-strung
ovum egg, cell

P

pachyderm elephant
pacifist one who opposes all violence
pacify appease
pact agreement
paean a song of praise
pagan heathen, ungodly
page attendant
pageant exhibition, show
pains great effort, attention to detail
painstaking taking great care, thorough
palatial grand, splendid
palaver babble, nonsense
Paleolithic stone age
paleontologist one who studies fossils
pall to become dull or weary
palliate assuage
pallid pale, sallow
palpable touchable
palpitate beat, throb
palsy paralysis
paltry scarce
pan criticize
panacea cure-all
panache flamboyance
pandemic widespread, plague
pandemonium din, commotion
pander cater to people's baser instincts
panegyric praise
pang short sharp pain
panoply full suit of armor
panorama vista
pant gasp, puff
pantomime mime
pantry storeroom

papyrus paper

parable allegory

paradigm a model

paragon standard of excellence

parameter limit

paramount chief, foremost

paramour lover

paranoid obsessively suspicious, demented

paranormal supernatural

parapet rampart, defense

paraphernalia equipment

paraphrase restatement

parcel package

parchment paper

pare peel

parenthetical in parentheses

pariah outcast

parish fold, church

parity equality

parlance local speech

parlay increase

parley conference

parochial provincial

parody imitation, ridicule

parole release

paroxysm outburst, convulsion

parrot mimic

parry avert, ward off

parsimonious stingy

parson clergyman

partake share, receive, consume

partial incomplete

partiality bias

parting farewell, severance

partisan supporter

partition division

parvenu newcomer, social climber

pasquinade satire

passé outmoded

passim here and there

pastel pale

pasteurize disinfect

pastoral rustic

patent obvious

paternal fatherly

pathetic pitiful

pathogen agent causing disease

pathogenic causing disease

pathos emotion

patrician aristocrat

patrimony inheritance

patronize condescend

patronymic a name formed form the name of a father

patter walk lightly

paucity scarcity

Quiz 23 (Matching)

Match each word in the first column with its definition in the second column. Answers are on page 101.

1. ORDNANCE
2. ORTHODOX
3. OUTMODED
4. PALAVER
5. PANEGYRIC
6. PARADIGM
7. PARLANCE
8. PAROXYSM
9. PARSIMONIOUS
10. PATHOGEN

A. a model
B. local speech
C. convulsion
D. stingy
E. agent causing disease
F. artillery
G. conventional
H. out-of-date
I. babble
J. praise

paunch stomach

pauper poor person

pavilion tent

pawn (noun) tool, stooge

pawn (verb) pledge

pax peace

peaked wan, pale, haggard

peal reverberation, outburst

peccadillo a minor fault

peculate embezzle

peculiar unusual

peculiarity characteristic

pedagogical pertaining to teaching

pedagogue dull, formal teacher

pedant pedagogue

pedantic bookish

peddle sell

pedestrian common

pedigree genealogy

peerage aristocracy

peevish cranky

pejorative insulting

pell-mell in a confused manner

pellucid transparent

pen write

penance atonement

penchant inclination

pend depend, hang

pending not decided, awaiting

penitent repentant

pensive sad

penurious stingy

penury poverty

peon common worker

per se in itself

perceptive discerning

percolate ooze, permeate

perdition damnation

peregrination wandering

peremptory dictatorial

perennial enduring, lasting
perfectionist purist, precisionist
perfidious treacherous (of a person)
perforate puncture
perforce by necessity
perfunctory careless
perigee point nearest to the earth
perilous dangerous
peripatetic walking about
periphery outer boundary
perish die
perishable decomposable
perjury lying
permeate spread throughout
permutation reordering
pernicious destructive, evil
peroration conclusion
perpendicular at right angles
perpetrate commit
perpetual continuous, everlasting
perpetuate cause to continue
perpetuity eternity
perplex puzzle, bewilder
perquisite reward, bonus
persecute harass
persevere persist, endure
persona social facade
personable charming, friendly
personage official, dignitary

personify embody, exemplify
personnel employees
perspicacious keen
perspicacity discernment, keenness
persuasive convincing
pert flippant, bold
pertain to relate
pertinacious persevering
pertinent relevant
perturbation agitation
peruse read carefully
pervade permeate
pessimist cynic, naysayer
pestilence disease
petite small
petition a written request
petrify calcify, shock
petrology study of rocks
pettifogger unscrupulous lawyer
petty trivial, niggling
petulant irritable, peevish
phantasm apparition
phenomena unusual natural events
philanthropic charitable
philanthropist altruist
philatelist stamp collector
philippic invective
Philistine barbarian
philosophical contemplative

Quiz 24 (Analogies)

Directions: Choose the pair that expresses a relationship most similar to that expressed in the capitalized pair. Answers are on page 101.

1. SECLUSION : HERMIT ::
   - (A) wealth: embezzler
   - (B) ambition : philanthropist
   - (C) domination : athlete
   - (D) turpitude : introvert
   - (E) injustice : lawyer

2. ASCETIC : SELF-DENIAL ::
   - (A) soldier : safety
   - (B) official : charity
   - (C) thug : acceptance
   - (D) benefactor : competition
   - (E) profligate : squandering

3. Philanthropist : Altruism ::
   - (A) authoritarian : indulgence
   - (B) polemicist : Marxist
   - (C) benefactor : heir
   - (D) pragmatist : hard-liner
   - (E) libertarian : liberty

4. RACONTEUR : ANECDOTE ::
   - (A) cynosure : interest
   - (B) politician : corruption
   - (C) athlete : perfection
   - (D) writer : publication
   - (E) nonentity : fame

5. PATENT : MANIFEST ::
   - (A) credulous : gullible
   - (B) truculent : nonchalant
   - (C) lissome : spiritless
   - (D) covert : prolific
   - (E) cloyed : insufficient

6. CENSORIOUS : CONDONING ::
   - (A) inattentive : neglectful
   - (B) cursory : inept
   - (C) defunct : exquisite
   - (D) perfunctory : thorough
   - (E) munificent : generous

7. PURGE : OPPONENT ::
   - (A) entrench : comrade
   - (B) elevate : criminal
   - (C) liquidate : politician
   - (D) desalinize : salt
   - (E) assuage : reactionary

8. ISLAND : ATOLL ::
   - (A) peninsula : archipelago
   - (B) fire : spring
   - (C) hand : glove
   - (D) utensil : fork
   - (E) smock : instrument

9. MNEMONIC : MEMORY ::
   - (A) demonstration : manifestation
   - (B) pacemaker : heartbeat
   - (C) sanction : recall
   - (D) rhetoric : treatise
   - (E) impasse : fruition

10. EAT : GORGE ::
    - (A) sprint : jog
    - (B) snicker : smirk
    - (C) read : write
    - (D) disengage : attack
    - (E) drink : guzzle

phlegmatic sluggish
phobia fear
phoenix rebirth

physic laxative, cathartic
physique frame, musculature
picaresque roguish, adventurous

picayune trifling
piecemeal one at a time
pied mottled, brindled
piety devoutness
pilfer steal
pillage plunder
pillory punish by ridicule
pine languish, to long for someone or something
pinnacle highest point
pious devout, holy
piquant tart-tasting, spicy
pique sting, arouse interest
piscine pertaining to fish
piteous sorrowful, pathetic
pithy concise
pitiable miserable, wretched
pittance alms, driblet
pittance trifle
pivotal crucial
pixilated eccentric, possessed
placard poster
placate appease
placid serene
plagiarize pirate, counterfeit
plaintive expressing sorrow
platitude trite remark
platonic nonsexual
plaudit acclaim
pleasantry banter, persiflage
plebeian common, vulgar
plebiscite referendum
plenary full
plentiful abundant
pleonasm redundancy, verbosity
plethora overabundance
pliable flexible
pliant supple, flexible
plight sad situation
plucky courageous
plumb measure
plummet sudden short fall
plutocrat wealthy person
plutonium radioactive material
poach steal
podgy fat
podium stand, rostrum
pogrom massacre, mass murder
poignant pungent, sharp, heartbreaking
polemic a controversy
polity methods of government
poltroon dastard
polychromatic many-colored
polygamist one who has many wives
ponder muse, reflect
ponderous heavy, bulky
pontiff bishop
pontificate to speak at length

pootroon coward

porcine pig-like

porous permeable, spongy

porridge stew

portend signify, augur

portent omen

portly large

portmanteau suitcase

posit stipulate

posterior rear, subsequent

posterity future generations

posthaste hastily

posthumous after death

postulate supposition, premise

potent powerful

potentate sovereign, king

potion brew

potpourri medley

potter aimlessly busy

pragmatic practical

prate babble

prattle chatter

preamble introduction

precarious dangerous, risky

precedent an act that serves as an example

precept principle, law

precinct neighborhood

precipice cliff

precipitate cause

precipitous steep

précis summary

precise accurate, detailed

preclude prevent

precocious more developed than is expected at a particular age

preconception prejudgment, prejudice

precursor forerunner

predacious plundering

predecessor one who proceeds

predestine foreordain

predicament quandary

predicate to base an opinion on something

predilection inclination

predisposed inclined

preeminent supreme

preempt commandeer

preen groom

prefabricated ready-built

prefect magistrate

preference choice

preferment promotion

prelate primate, bishop

preliminary introductory

prelude introduction

premeditate plan in advance

premonition warning

prenatal before birth

Quiz 25 (Matching)

Match each word in the first column with its definition in the second column. Answers are on page 102.

1. PHOENIX
2. PILLORY
3. PITTANCE
4. PLAUDIT
5. PLETHORA
6. POGROM
7. POSTHUMOUS
8. PRECIPICE
9. PREDILECTION
10. PREMONITION

A. cliff
B. inclination
C. warning
D. acclaim
E. overabundance
F. after death
G. massacre
H. rebirth
I. punish by ridicule
J. trifle

preponderance predominance

prepossessing appealing, charming

preposterous ridiculous

prerequisite requirement

prerogative right, privilege

presage omen

prescribe urge

presentable acceptable, well-mannered

preside direct, chair

pressing urgent

prestidigitator magician

prestige reputation, renown

presume assume, deduce

presumptuous assuming, overconfident

presuppose assume

pretense affectation, excuse

pretentious affected, inflated

preternatural abnormal, supernatural

pretext excuse

prevail triumph

prevailing common, current

prevalent widespread

prevaricate lie

prick puncture

priggish pedantic, affected

prim formal, prudish

primal first, beginning

primate head, master

primogeniture first-born child

primp groom

princely regal, generous

prismatic many-colored, sparkling

pristine pure, unspoiled

privation hardship

privy aware of private matters

probe examine

probity integrity

problematic uncertain, difficult

proboscis snout

procedure method, process

proceeds profit
proclaim announce
proclivity inclination
procreate beget
proctor supervise
procure acquire
procurer pander
prod urge
prodigal wasteful
prodigious marvelous, enormous
prodigy a person with extraordinary ability or talent
profane blasphemous
profess affirm, admit
proffer bring forward for consideration
proficient skillful
profiteer extortionist
profligate licentious, prodigal
profound deep, knowledgeable
profusion overabundance
progenitor ancestor
progeny children
prognosis forecast
prognosticate foretell
progressive advancing, liberal
proletariat working class
proliferate increase rapidly
prolific fruitful, productive
prolix long-winded

prologue introduction
prolong lengthen in time
promenade stroll, parade
promethean inspirational
promiscuous sexually indiscreet
promontory headland, cape
prompt induce
prompter reminder
promulgate publish, disseminate
prone inclined, predisposed
propaganda publicity, misinformation
propellant rocket fuel
propensity inclination
prophet prognosticator
prophylactic preventive
propinquity nearness
propitiate satisfy
propitious auspicious, favorable
proponent supporter, advocate
proportionate commensurate
proposition offer, proposal
propound propose
proprietor manager, owner
propriety decorum
prosaic uninspired, flat
proscenium platform, rostrum
proscribe prohibit
proselytize recruit, convert
prosody study of poetic structure

Quiz 26 (Analogies)

Directions: Choose the pair that expresses a relationship most similar to that expressed in the capitalized pair. Answers are on page 102.

1. CALLOUS : SYMPATHY ::
    - (A) flawless : excellence
    - (B) histrionic : theatrics
    - (C) outgoing : inhibition
    - (D) indiscreet : platitude
    - (E) categorical : truism

2. INSIPID : TASTE ::
    - (A) curt : incivility
    - (B) apathetic : zest
    - (C) immaculate : brevity
    - (D) trite : unimportance
    - (E) discriminating : scholarship

3. Apocryphal : Corroboration ::
    - (A) didactic : instruction
    - (B) fraudulent : forgery
    - (C) tyrannical : poise
    - (D) esoteric : commonality
    - (E) sacrilegious : piety

4. NEBULOUS : DISTINCTION ::
    - (A) guileless : deceit
    - (B) antipathetic : abhorrence
    - (C) sublime : disrespect
    - (D) magnanimous : anxiety
    - (E) amorphous : inchoation

5. TARNISH : VITIATE ::
    - (A) beleaguer : console
    - (B) abrogate : flicker
    - (C) ensconce : corrupt
    - (D) bemuse : stupefy
    - (E) inundate : squelch

6. NOCTURNAL : CIMMERIAN ::
    - (A) exacting : lax
    - (B) prudish : indulgent
    - (C) contentious : affluent
    - (D) stark : embellished
    - (E) specious : illusory

7. CONVOCATION : MEETING ::
    - (A) bargain : market
    - (B) supplication : prayer
    - (C) issue : referendum
    - (D) speech : podium
    - (E) harvest : fall

8. OSTRICH : BIRD ::
    - (A) dusk : day
    - (B) fish : ocean
    - (C) tunnel : mountain
    - (D) hat : coat
    - (E) sirocco : storm

9. VIRUS : ORGANISM ::
    - (A) vegetable : mineral
    - (B) test-tube : bacteria
    - (C) microcosm : world
    - (D) microfiche : computer
    - (E) watch : wrist

10. Mercurial : Temperament ::
    - (A) capricious : interest
    - (B) tempestuous : solemnity
    - (C) staid : wantonness
    - (D) phlegmatic : concern
    - (E) cynical : naiveté

prospective expected, imminent
prospectus brochure
prostrate supine

protagonist main character in a story
protean changing readily
protégé ward, pupil

protocol code of diplomatic etiquette
proton particle
protract prolong
protuberance bulge
provender food
proverb maxim
proverbial well-known
providence foresight, divine protection
provident having foresight, thrifty
providential fortunate
province bailiwick, district
provincial intolerant, insular
provisional temporary
proviso stipulation
provisory conditional
provocation incitement
provocative titillating
provoke incite
prowess strength, expertise
proximity nearness
proxy substitute, agent
prude puritan
prudence discretion, carefulness
prudent cautious, using good judgment
prudish puritanical
prurient lewd
pseudo false
pseudonym alias

psychic pertaining the psyche or mind
psychopath madman
psychotic demented
puberty adolescence
puckish impish, mischievous
puerile childish
pugilism boxing
pugnacious combative
puissant strong
pulchritude beauty
pulp paste, mush
pulpit platform, priesthood
pulsate throb
pulverize crush
pun wordplay
punctilious meticulous
pundit learned or politically astute person
pungent sharp smell or taste
punitive punishing
puny weak, small
purblind obtuse, stupid
purgative cathartic, cleansing
purgatory limbo, netherworld
purge cleanse, remove
puritanical prim
purlieus environs, surroundings
purloin steal
purport claim to be

purported rumored
purposeful determined
pursuant following, according
purvey deliver, provide
purview range of understanding, field
pusillanimous cowardly
putative reputed
putrefy decay
putsch a sudden attempt to overthrow a government
pygmy dwarf
pyrotechnics fireworks
pyrrhic a battle won with unacceptable losses

Q

quack charlatan
quadrennial occurring every four years
quadrille square dance
quadruped four foot animal
quaff drink
quagmire difficult situation
quail shrink, cower
quaint old-fashioned, charming
qualified limited
qualms misgivings
quandary dilemma
quantum quantity, particle
quarantine detention, confinement

quarry prey, game
quarter residence, district
quash put down, suppress
quasi seeming, almost
quaver tremble
quay wharf
queasy squeamish
queer odd
quell suppress, allay
quench extinguish, slake
querulous complaining
questionnaire survey, feedback
queue line
quibble bicker
quicken revive, hasten
quiddity essence, an unimportant or trifling distinction
quiescent still, motionless
quietus a cessation of activity
quill feather, pen
quip joke
quirk eccentricity, a strange and unexpected turn of events
quiver tremble
quixotic impractical, romantic
quizzical odd, questioning
quorum the minimum number people who must be present to hold a meeting
quota a share or proportion
quotidian daily

Quiz 27 (Matching)

Match each word in the first column with its definition in the second column.
Answers are on page 102.

1. PROTEAN
2. PROTUBERANCE
3. PROVISIONAL
4. PUNDIT
5. PURLOIN
6. PURPORT
7. QUAVER
8. QUEUE
9. QUIETUS
10. QUORUM

A. bulge
B. changing readily
C. steal
D. majority
E. temporary
F. a cessation of activity
G. line
H. tremble
I. claim to be
J. politically astute person

R

rabble crowd

rabid mad, furious

racketeer gangster, swindler

raconteur storyteller

radical revolutionary

raffish rowdy, dashing

rail rant, harangue

raiment clothing

rake womanizer

rally assemble

rambunctious boisterous

ramification consequence

rampage run amuck

rampant unbridled, raging

ramrod rod

rancid rotten

rancor resentment

randy vulgar

rankle cause bitterness, resentment

rant rage, scold

rapacious grasping, avaricious

rapidity speed

rapier sword

rapine plunder

rapport affinity, empathy

rapprochement reconciliation

rapture bliss

rash hasty, brash

rasp scrape

ratify approve

ration allowance, portion

rationale justification

ravage plunder, ruin

ravish captivate, charm

raze destroy or level a building

realm kingdom, domain

realpolitik cynical interpretation of politics

reap harvest

rebuff reject, snub

rebuke criticize, reprimand

rebus picture puzzle

rebuttal reply, counterargument

recalcitrant stubbornly resisting the authority of another

recant retract a previous statement

recapitulate restate, summarize

recede move back

receptacle container

receptive open to ideas

recidivism habitual criminal activity

recipient one who receives

reciprocal mutual, return in kind

recital performance, concert

recitation recital, lesson

reclusive solitary

recoil flinch, retreat

recollect remember

recompense repay, compensate

reconcile adjust, balance

recondite mystical, profound

reconnaissance surveillance

reconnoiter to survey, to scout (especially for military purposes)

recount recite

recoup recover

recourse appeal, resort

recreant cowardly

recrimination countercharge, retaliation

recruit draftee

rectify correct, to make right

recumbent reclining

recuperation recovery

recur repeat, revert

redeem buy back, justify, restore yourself to favor or to good opinion

redeemer savior

redemption salvation

redolent fragrant

redoubt fort

redoubtable formidable, steadfast

redress restitution, compensation

redundant repetitious

reek smell

reel stagger, to lurch backward as though struck by a blow

referendum vote

refined purified, cultured

reflux ebb

refraction bending, deflection

refractory obstinate, disobedient

refrain abstain

refurbish remodel, renovate

refute disprove, contradict

regal royal

regale entertain

regalia emblems

Quiz 28 (Analogies)

<u>Directions:</u> Choose the pair that expresses a relationship most similar to that expressed in the capitalized pair. Answers are on page 102.

1. PLUMMET : FALL ::
   - (A) rifle : search
   - (B) accelerate : stop
   - (C) interdict : proscribe
   - (D) rake : scour
   - (E) precipitate : ascend

2. DRONE : EMOTION ::
   - (A) sprint : journey
   - (B) annoy : emollient
   - (C) stupefy : erudition
   - (D) deadpan : expression
   - (E) scuttle : ship

3. MAROON : SEQUESTER ::
   - (A) transfix : emote
   - (B) exhaust : innervate
   - (C) tranquilize : qualify
   - (D) select : rebuff
   - (E) entreat : beseech

4. TOTTER : WALK ::
   - (A) annex : land
   - (B) fathom : enlightenment
   - (C) distend : contusion
   - (D) efface : consolation
   - (E) stutter : speech

5. LIGHT : DIM ::
   - (A) indictment : investigate
   - (B) protest : muffle
   - (C) heat : radiate
   - (D) solid : incinerate
   - (E) ornament : decorate

6. BENIGN : PERNICIOUS ::
   - (A) ostentatious : tawdry
   - (B) mortified : nefarious
   - (C) apocryphal : categorical
   - (D) discerning : keen
   - (E) pejorative : vicarious

7. Demagogue : Manipulator ::
   - (A) champion : defender
   - (B) lawyer : mediator
   - (C) mentor : oppressor
   - (D) soldier : landowner
   - (E) capitalist : socialist

8. GREGARIOUS : CONGENIAL ::
   - (A) suspicious : trusting
   - (B) pedantic : lively
   - (C) bellicose : militant
   - (D) singular : nondescript
   - (E) seminal : apocalyptic

9. DISHEARTENED : HOPE ::
   - (A) enervated : ennui
   - (B) buoyant : effervescence
   - (C) amoral : ethics
   - (D) munificent : altruism
   - (E) nefarious : turpitude

10. PRATTLE : SPEAK ::
    - (A) accept : reject
    - (B) stomp : patter
    - (C) heed : listen
    - (D) promenade : walk
    - (E) ejaculate : shout

regime a government
regiment infantry unit
regrettable lamentable, unfortunate
regurgitate vomit, repeat
rehash wearily discuss again
reign rule, influence

rein curb, restrain

reincarnation rebirth

reiterate repeat, say again

rejoice celebrate

rejoinder answer, retort

rejuvenate make young again

relapse recurrence (of illness)

relegate assign to an inferior position

relent soften, yield

relentless unstoppable

relic antique

relinquish release, renounce

relish savor

remedial corrective

remiss negligent

remit forgive, send payment

remnant residue, fragment

remonstrance protest

remorse guilt

remuneration compensation

renaissance rebirth

renascent reborn

rend to tear apart

render deliver, provide

rendezvous a meeting

rendition version, interpretation

renege break a promise

renounce disown

renown fame

rent tear, rupture

reparation amends, atonement

repartee witty conversation

repatriate to send back to the native land

repellent causing aversion

repent atone for

repercussion consequence

repertoire stock of works

repine fret

replenish refill

replete complete

replica copy

replicate duplicate

repose rest

reprehensible blameworthy

repress suppress

reprieve temporary suspension

reprimand rebuke

reprisal retaliation

reprise repetition

reproach blame

reprobate miscreant

reprove rebuke

repudiate disavow

repugnant distasteful, revolting

repulse repel

repulsive repugnant

repute status, reputation, esteem

reputed supposed, presumed, alleged
requiem rest, a mass for the dead
requisite necessary
requisition order, formal demand
requite to return in kind
rescind revoke
reserve self-control
reside dwell
residue remaining part
resigned accepting of a situation
resilience ability to recover from an illness or a setback
resolute determined
resolution determination
resolve determination
resonant reverberating
resort recourse
resound echo
resourceful inventive, skillful
respectively in that order
respire breathe
respite rest, temporary delay
resplendent shining, splendid
restitution reparation, amends
restive nervous, uneasy
resurgence revival
resurrection rebirth
resuscitate revive
retain keep

retainer advance fee
retaliate revenge
retch vomit
reticent reserved
retiring modest, unassuming
retort quick reply
retrench cut back, economize
retribution reprisal
retrieve reclaim
retrograde regress
retrospective reminiscent, display
revamp recast
reveille bugle call
revel frolic, take joy in
revelry merrymaking
revenue income
revere honor
reverent respectful
reverie daydream
revert return to a former state
revile denounce, defame
revision new version
revive renew
revoke repeal
revulsion aversion
rhapsody ecstasy
rhetoric elocution, grandiloquence
rheumatism inflammation
ribald coarse, vulgar

Quiz 29 (Matching)

Match each word in the first column with its definition in the second column. Answers are on page 102.

1. REGIME
2. REJOINDER
3. REMUNERATION
4. RENDEZVOUS
5. RENT
6. REPROBATE
7. REQUISITE
8. RESTIVE
9. RETRIBUTION
10. RIBALD

A. vulgar
B. quick reply
C. uneasy
D. necessary
E. miscreant
F. rupture
G. a meeting
H. compensation
I. retort
J. a government

rickety shaky, ramshackle

ricochet carom, rebound

rife widespread, abundant

riffraff dregs of society

rifle search through and steal

rift a split, an opening, disagreement

righteous upright, moral

rigor harshness, precise and exacting

rime crust

riposte counterthrust

risible laughable

risqué off-color, racy

rivet engross

robust vigorous

rogue scoundrel

roister bluster

romp frolic

roseate rosy, optimistic

roster list of people

rostrum podium

roué libertine

rouse awaken, provoke

rout vanquish, cause to retreat

rubicund ruddy complexion

ruck the common herd

rudiment beginning, kernel

rue regret

ruffian brutal person

ruminate ponder

rummage hunt, grope

runel stream

ruse trick

rustic rural

S

Sabbath day of rest

sabbatical vacation

saber sword

sabotage treason, destruction

saccharine sugary, overly sweet tone

sacerdotal priestly

sack pillage

sacrament rite

sacred cow idol, taboo

sacrilege blasphemy

sacrosanct sacred

saddle encumber

sadist one who takes pleasure in hurting others

safari expedition

saga story

sagacious wise

sage wise person

salacious licentious

salient prominent

saline salty

sallow sickly complected

sally sortie, attack

salutary good, wholesome

salutation salute, greeting

salvation redemption

salve medicinal ointment

salvo volley, gunfire

sanctify consecrate

sanctimonious self-righteous

sanction approval

sanctuary refuge

sang-froid coolness under fire

sanguinary gory, murderous

sanguine cheerful

sans without

sapid interesting

sapient wise

sarcophagus stone coffin

scornful contemptuous

sartorial pertaining to clothes

satanic pertaining to the Devil

satchel bag

sate satisfy fully

satiate satisfy fully

satire ridicule

saturate soak

saturnine gloomy

satyr demigod, goat-man

saunter stroll

savanna grassland

savant scholar

savoir-faire tact, polish

savor enjoy, relish

savory appetizing

savvy perceptive, shrewd

scabrous difficult

scant inadequate, meager

scapegoat one who takes blame for others

scarify criticize

scathe injure, denounce

Quiz 30 (Analogies)

Directions: Choose the pair that expresses a relationship most similar to that expressed in the capitalized pair. Answers are on page 102.

1. THIMBLE : FINGER ::
   - (A) glove : hammer
   - (B) stitch : loop
   - (C) branch : flower
   - (D) talon : eagle
   - (E) smock : apparel

2. ANARCHY : ORDER ::
   - (A) desolation : annihilation
   - (B) ineptitude : skill
   - (C) bastion : aegis
   - (D) chaos : disarray
   - (E) parsimony : elegance

3. LAND : FALLOW ::
   - (A) automobile : expensive
   - (B) politics : innovative
   - (C) orchard : fruitful
   - (D) mountain : precipitous
   - (E) ship : decommissioned

4. HEURISTIC : TEACH ::
   - (A) parable : obfuscate
   - (B) performer : entertain
   - (C) pedant : construct
   - (D) actor : incite
   - (E) virus : prevent

5. RUSE : DECEIVE ::
   - (A) pretext : mollify
   - (B) invective : laud
   - (C) cathartic : cleanse
   - (D) artifice : disabuse
   - (E) calumny : confuse

6. RETICENT : WANTON ::
   - (A) lithe : supple
   - (B) exemplary : palpable
   - (C) pejorative : opprobrious
   - (D) quiescent : rampant
   - (E) provincial : virulent

7. GULLIBLE : DUPE ::
   - (A) artless : demagogue
   - (B) Machiavellian : entrepreneur
   - (C) cantankerous : curmudgeon
   - (D) disputatious : patron
   - (E) optimistic : defeatist

8. OPAQUE : LIGHT ::
   - (A) porous : liquid
   - (B) undamped : vibration
   - (C) unrelenting : barbarian
   - (D) diaphanous : metal
   - (E) hermetic : air

9. QUIXOTIC : PRAGMATIC ::
   - (A) romantic : fanciful
   - (B) dispassionate : just
   - (C) auspicious : sanguine
   - (D) malcontent : jingoistic
   - (E) optimistic : surreal

10. COLON : INTRODUCE ::
    - (A) hyphen : join
    - (B) semicolon : transfer
    - (C) dash : shorten
    - (D) apostrophe : intensify
    - (E) comma : possess

scepter a rod, staff
scheme plot, system, diagram
schism rift
scintilla speck
scintillate sparkle
scion offspring

scoff jeer, dismiss
scone biscuit
scorn disdain, reject
scoundrel unprincipled person
scour clean by rubbing, search
scourge affliction
scruples misgivings
scrupulous principled, fastidious
scrutinize examine closely
scurf dandruff
scurrilous abusive, insulting
scurry move quickly
scuttle to sink (a ship)
scythe long, curved blade
sear burn
sebaceous like fat
secede withdraw
secluded remote, isolated
seclusion solitude
sectarian denominational
secular worldly, nonreligious
secure make safe
sedation state of calm
sedentary stationary, inactive
sedition treason, inciting rebellion
seduce lure
sedulous diligent
seedy rundown, ramshackle
seemly proper, attractive

seethe fume, resent
seismic pertaining to earthquakes
seismology study of earthquakes
self-effacing modest
semantics study of word meanings
semblance likeness
seminal fundamental, decisive
semper fidelis always loyal
senescence old age
senescent aging
seniority privilege due to length of service
sensational outstanding, startling
sensible wise, prudent
sensory relating to the senses
sensualist epicure
sensuous appealing to the senses, enjoying luxury
sententious concise
sentient conscious
sentinel watchman
sepulcher tomb
sequacious dependent
sequel continuation, epilogue
sequester segregate
seraphic angelic
serendipity a knack for making fortunate discoveries
serene peaceful
serpentine winding and twisting

serried saw-toothed
serum vaccine
servile slavish
servitude forced labor
sessile permanently attached
session meeting
settee seat, sofa
sever cut in two
severance division
shallot onion
sham pretense, imposter
shambles disorder, mess
shard sharp fragment of glass
sheen luster
sheepish shy, embarrassed
shibboleth password
shirk evade (work)
sliver fragment, shaving
shoal reef
shoring supporting
shortcomings personal deficiencies
shrew virago
shrewd clever, cunning
shrill high-pitched
shun avoid, spurn
shunt turn aside
shyster unethical lawyer
sibilant a hissing sound
sibling brother or sister

sickle semicircular blade
sidereal pertaining to the stars
sidle move sideways, slither
siege blockade
sierra mountain range
sieve strainer
signatory signer
signet a seal
silhouette outline, profile
silo storage tower
simian monkey
simile figure of speech
simper smile, smirk
simulacrum vague likeness
sinecure position with little responsibility
sinewy fibrous, stringy
singe burn just the surface of something
singly one by one, individually
singular unique, extraordinary
sinister evil, malicious
sinistral left-handed
siphon extract, tap
sire forefather, to beget
siren temptress
site location
skeptical doubtful
skinflint miser
skirmish a small battle

Quiz 31 (Matching)

Match each word in the first column with its definition in the second column. Answers are on page 102.

1. SCRUPLES
2. SCYTHE
3. SEEMLY
4. SENTENTIOUS
5. SERENDIPITY
6. SHIBBOLETH
7. SIDEREAL
8. SIGNATORY
9. SIMILE
10. SINISTRAL

A. figure of speech
B. proper, attractive
C. long, curved blade
D. left-handed
E. pertaining to the stars
F. signer
G. making fortunate discoveries
H. password
I. misgivings
J. concise

skittish excitable, wary, jumpy

skulk sneak about

skullduggery trickery

slake quench

slander defame

slate list of candidate

slaver drivel, fawn

slay kill

sleight dexterity, skill

slew an abundance

slither slide, slink

slogan motto

sloth laziness

slovenly sloppy

smattering superficial knowledge

smelt refine metal

smirk smug look

smite strike, afflict

smock apron

snare trap

snide sarcastic, spiteful

snippet morsel, small piece

snivel whine, sniff

snub ignore, slight

snuff extinguish

sobriety composed, abstinent, sober

sobriquet nickname

socialite one who is prominent in society

sociology study of society

sodality companionship

sodden soaked

sojourn trip, stopover

solace consolation, comfort

solder fuse, weld

solecism ungrammatical construction

solemn serious, somber

solemnity seriousness

solicit request

solicitous considerate, concerned
soliloquy monologue
solstice furthest point
soluble dissolvable
solvent financially sound
somatic pertaining to the body
somber gloomy, solemn
somnambulist sleepwalker
somnolent sleepy
sonnet short poem
sonorous resonant, majestic
sop morsel, compensation, offering
sophistry specious reasoning
soporific sleep inducing
soprano high female voice
sordid foul, ignoble
sorority sisterhood
soubrette actress, ingenue
souse a drunk
sovereign monarch
spar fight
spasmodic intermittent, fitful
spate sudden outpouring
spawn produce
specimen sample
specious false but plausible reasoning
spectacle public display
spectral ghostly
spectrum range, gamut

speculate conjecture
speleologist one who studies caves
spew eject
spindle shaft
spindly tall and thin
spinster old maid
spire pinnacle
spirited lively
spirituous alcohol, intoxicating
spite malice, grudge
spittle spit
splay spread apart
spleen resentment, wrath
splenetic peevish
splurge indulge
spontaneous extemporaneous
sporadic occurring irregularly
sportive playful
spry nimble
spume foam, froth
spurious false, counterfeit
spurn to reject a person with scorn
squalid filthy
squall rain storm
squander waste
squelch crush, stifle
stagnant stale, motionless
staid demure, sedate

Quiz 32 (Analogies)

Directions: Choose the pair that expresses a relationship most similar to that expressed in the capitalized pair. Answers are on page 102.

1. PERSPICACIOUS : INSIGHT ::
   - (A) ardent : quickness
   - (B) warm : temperature
   - (C) wealthy : scarcity
   - (D) rapacious : magnanimity
   - (E) churlish : enmity

2. Unprecedented : Previous Occurrence ::
   - (A) naive : harmony
   - (B) incomparable : equal
   - (C) improper : vacillation
   - (D) eccentric : intensity
   - (E) random : recidivism

3. SNAKE : INVERTEBRATE ::
   - (A) dolphin : fish
   - (B) eagle : talon
   - (C) boa constrictor : backbone
   - (D) penguin : bird
   - (E) bat : insect

4. LIMERICK : POEM ::
   - (A) monologue : chorus
   - (B) sonnet : offering
   - (C) waltz : tango
   - (D) skull : skeleton
   - (E) aria : song

5. INTEREST : OBSESSION ::
   - (A) faith : caprice
   - (B) nonchalance : insouciance
   - (C) diligence : assiduity
   - (D) decimation : annihilation
   - (E) alacrity : procrastination

6. RESOLUTE : WILL ::
   - (A) violent : peacefulness
   - (B) fanatic : concern
   - (C) balky : contrary
   - (D) notorious : infamy
   - (E) virtuous : wholesomeness

7. ATOM : MATTER ::
   - (A) neutron : proton
   - (B) vegetable : animal
   - (C) molecule : element
   - (D) component : system
   - (E) pasture : herd

8. ACTORS : TROUPE ::
   - (A) plotters : cabal
   - (B) professors : tenure
   - (C) workers : bourgeoisie
   - (D) diplomats : government
   - (E) directors : cast

9. COFFER : VALUABLES ::
   - (A) mountain : avalanche
   - (B) book : paper
   - (C) vault : trifles
   - (D) sanctuary : refuge
   - (E) sea : waves

10. LION : CARNIVORE ::
    - (A) man : vegetarian
    - (B) ape : ponderer
    - (C) lizard : mammal
    - (D) buffalo : omnivore
    - (E) shark : scavenger

stalwart pillar, strong, loyal
stamina vigor, endurance
stanch loyal
stanchion prop, foundation
stanza division of a poem
stark desolate

startle surprise
stately impressive, noble
static inactive, immobile
statue regulation
staunch loyal
stave ward off
steadfast loyal
stealth secrecy, covertness
steeped soaked, infused
stenography shorthand
stentorian loud or declamatory in tone
sterling high quality
stern strict
stevedore longshoreman
stifle suppress
stigma mark of disgrace
stiletto dagger
stilted formal, stiff
stimulate excite
stint limit, assignment
stipend payment
stipulate specify, arrange
stodgy stuffy, pompous
stoic indifferent to pain or pleasure
stoke prod, fuel
stole long scarf
stolid impassive
stout stocky
strait distress

stratagem trick, military tactic
stratify form into layers
stratum layer
striate to mark with stripes
stricture censure, restriction
strife conflict
striking impressive, attractive
stringent severe, strict
strive endeavor
studious diligent
stultify inhibit, enfeeble
stunted arrested development
stupefy deaden, dumfound
stupendous astounding
stupor lethargy
stylize formalize, artificial artistic style
stymie hinder, thwart
suave smooth, charming
sub rosa in secret
subcutaneous beneath the skin
subdue conquer
subjugate suppress
sublet subcontract
sublimate to redirect forbidden impulses (usually sexual) into socially accepted activities
sublime lofty, excellent
sublunary earthly
submit yield, acquiesce
subordinate lower in rank

subsequent succeeding, following
subservient servile, submissive
subside diminish
subsidiary subordinate
subsidize financial assistance
substantiate verify
substantive substantial
subterfuge cunning, ruse
subterranean underground
subvert undermine
succor help, comfort
succulent juicy, delicious
succumb yield, submit
suffice adequate
suffrage vote
suffuse pervade, permeate
suggestive thought-provoking, risqué
sullen sulky, sour
sully stain
sultry sweltering
summon call for, arraign
sumptuous opulent, luscious
sunder split
sundry various
superb excellent
supercilious arrogant
supererogatory wanton, superfluous
superfluous overabundant
superimpose cover, place on top of

superintend supervise
superlative superior
supernumerary subordinate
supersede supplant
supervene ensue, follow
supervise oversee
supine lying on the back
supplant replace
supplication prayer
suppress subdue
surfeit overabundance
surly rude, crass
surmise to guess
surmount overcome
surname family name
surpass exceed, excel
surreal dreamlike
surreptitious secretive
surrogate substitute
surveillance close watch
susceptible vulnerable
suspend stop temporarily
sustenance food
susurrant whispering
suture surgical stitch
svelte slender
swank fashionable
swarthy dark (as in complexion)

Quiz 33 (Matching)

Match each word in the first column with its definition in the second column. Answers are on page 102.

1. STAVE
2. STEVEDORE
3. STRAIT
4. STUDIOUS
5. SUBJUGATE
6. SUBTERFUGE
7. SUNDRY
8. SUPERFLUOUS
9. SUPINE
10. SURREAL

A. distress
B. diligent
C. ward off
D. longshoreman
E. various
F. overabundant
G. suppress
H. cunning
I. dreamlike
J. lying on the back

swatch strip of fabric
sweltering hot
swivel a pivot
sybarite pleasure-seeker
sycophant flatterer, flunky
syllabicate divide into syllables
syllabus schedule
sylph a slim, graceful girl
sylvan rustic
symbiotic cooperative, working in close association
symmetry harmony, congruence
symposium panel (discussion)
symptomatic indicative
synagogue temple
syndicate cartel
syndrome set of symptoms
synod council
synopsis brief summary
synthesis combination
systole heart contraction

T

tabernacle temple
table postpone
tableau scene, backdrop
taboo prohibition
tabulate arrange
tacit understood without being spoken
taciturn untalkative
tactful sensitive
tactics strategy
tactile tangible
taint pollute
talion punishment
tally count
talon claw
tandem two or more things together
tang strong taste
tangential peripheral
tangible touchable

tantalize tease
tantamount equivalent
taper candle
tariff tax on imported or exported goods
tarn small lake
tarnish taint
tarry linger
taurine bull-like
taut tight
tautological repetitious
tawdry gaudy
technology body of knowledge
tedious boring, tiring
teem swarm, abound
temerity boldness
temperate moderate
tempest storm
tempestuous agitated
tempo speed
temporal pertaining to time
tempt entice
tenable defensible, valid
tenacious persistent
tendentious biased
tenement decaying apartment building
tenet doctrine
tensile stretchable
tentative provisional
tenuous thin, insubstantial
tenure status given after a period of time
tepid lukewarm
terminal final
terminology nomenclature
ternary triple
terpsichorean related to dance
terrain the feature of land
terrapin turtle
terrestrial earthly
terse concise
testament covenant
testy petulant
tether tie down
theatrics histrionics
theologian one who studies religion
thesaurus book of synonyms
thesis proposition, topic
thespian actor
thews muscles
thorny difficult
thrall slave
threadbare tattered
thrive prosper
throes anguish
throng crowd
throttle choke
thwart to foil

Quiz 34 (Matching)

Match each word in the first column with its definition in the second column. Answers are on page 102.

1. SWATCH
2. SYNOD
3. TACIT
4. TALON
5. TAURINE
6. TEMPESTUOUS
7. TENTATIVE
8. TERSE
9. THROES
10. THWART

A. to foil
B. anguish
C. concise
D. provisional
E. agitated
F. bull-like
G. claw
H. understood without being spoken
I. council
J. strip of fabric

tiara crown

tidings news, information

tiff fight

timbre tonal quality, resonance

timorous fearful, timid

tincture trace, vestige, tint

tinsel tawdriness

tirade scolding speech

titan accomplished person

titanic huge

titer laugh nervously

tithe donate one-tenth

titian auburn

titillate arouse

titular in name only, figurehead

toady fawner, sycophant

tocsin alarm bell, signal

toil drudgery

tome large book

tonal pertaining to sound

topography science of map making

torment harass

torpid lethargic, inactive

torrid scorching, passionate

torsion twisting

torus doughnut shaped object

totter stagger

touchstone standard

tousled disheveled

tout praise, brag

toxicologist one who studies poisons

tractable docile, manageable

traduce slander

tranquilize calm, anesthetize

transcribe write a copy

transfigure transform, exalt

transfix impale

transfuse insert, infuse

transgression trespass, offense

transient fleeting, temporary

transitory fleeting
translucent clear, lucid
transpire happen
transpose interchange
trauma injury
travail work, drudgery
traverse cross
travesty caricature, farce
treatise book, dissertation
trek journey
trenchant incisive, penetrating
trepidation fear
triad group of three
tribunal court
tributary river
trite commonplace, insincere
troglodyte cave dweller
trollop harlot
troublous disturbed
trounce thrash
troupe group of actors
truckle yield
truculent fierce, savage
trudge march, slog
truism self-evident truth
truncate shorten
truncheon club
tryst meeting, rendezvous
tumbler drinking glass

tumefy swell
tumult commotion
turbid muddy, clouded
turgid swollen
turpitude depravity
tussle fight
tussock cluster of glass
tutelage guardianship
twain two
twinge pain
tyrannical dictatorial
tyranny oppression
tyro beginner

U

ubiquitous omnipresent, pervasive
ulterior hidden, covert
ultimatum demand
ululate howl, wail
umbrage resentment
unabashed shameless, brazen
unabated ceaseless
unaffected natural, sincere
unanimity agreement
unassuming modest
unavailing useless, futile
unawares suddenly, unexpectedly
unbecoming unfitting
unbridled unrestrained

Quiz 35 (Matching)

Match each word in the first column with its definition in the second column. Answers are on page 102.

1. TIDINGS
2. TITER
3. TITULAR
4. TORPID
5. TRADUCE
6. TRENCHANT
7. UBIQUITOUS
8. ULULATE
9. UNABATED
10. UNBRIDLED

A. incisive
B. omnipresent
C. lethargic
D. figurehead
E. unrestrained
F. news
G. laugh nervously
H. ceaseless
I. wail
J. slander

uncanny mysterious, inexplicable

unconscionable unscrupulous

uncouth uncultured, crude

unctuous insincere

undermine weaken

underpin support

underscore emphasize

understudy a stand-in

underworld criminal world

underwrite agree to finance, guarantee

undue unjust, excessive

undulate surge, fluctuate

unduly excessive

unequivocal unambiguous, categorical

unexceptionable beyond criticism

unfailing steadfast, unfaltering

unfathomable puzzling, incomprehensible

unflagging untiring, unrelenting

unflappable not easily upset

unfrock discharge

unfurl open up, spread out

ungainly awkward

uniformity sameness

unilateral action taken by only one party

unimpeachable exemplary

unison together

unkempt disheveled

unmitigated complete, harsh

unmoved firm, steadfast

unprecedented without previous occurrence

unremitting relentless

unsavory distasteful, offensive

unscathed unhurt

unseat displace

unseemly unbecoming, improper

unstinting generous

unsullied spotless, pure

unsung neglected, not receiving just recognition

untenable cannot be achieved

untoward perverse, unseemly

unwarranted unjustified

unwieldy awkward

unwitting unintentional

upshot result

urbane refined, worldly

ursine bear-like

usurp seize, to appropriate

usury lending money at high rates

utilitarian pragmatic, useful

utopia paradise

utter complete

uxorious a doting husband

V

vacillate waver

vacuous inane, empty

vagary whim

vain unsuccessful

vainglorious conceited

valediction farewell speech

valiant brave

validate affirm, authenticate

valor bravery

vanguard leading position

vanquish conquer

vapid vacuous, insipid

variance discrepancy

vassal subject, subordinate

vaunt brag

vehement adamant

venal mercenary, for the sake of money

vendetta grudge, feud

veneer false front, facade

venerable revered

venial excusable

venom poison, spite

venture risk, speculate

venturesome bold, risky

venue location

veracity truthfulness

veranda porch

verbatim word for word, literal

verbose wordy

verdant green, lush

verdict decision, judgment

vernacular common speech

vertigo dizziness

vestige trace, remnant

veto reject

vex annoy

viable capable of surviving, feasible

viaduct waterway

Quiz 36 (Matching)

Match each word in the first column with its definition in the second column. Answers are on page 102.

1. UNCOUTH
2. UNDULY
3. UNFLAGGING
4. UNKEMPT
5. UNSTINTING
6. UNTENABLE
7. UNWIELDY
8. VAGARY
9. VERACITY
10. VIABLE

A. disheveled
B. capable of surviving
C. awkward
D. uncultured
E. truthfulness
F. whim
G. unrelenting
H. cannot be achieved
I. generous
J. excessive

viand food

vicious evil, cruel

vicissitude changing fortunes

victuals food

vie compete

vigil watch, sentry duty

vigilant on guard

vignette scene

vigor vitality

vilify defame, malign

vindicate free from blame

vindictive revengeful

virile manly, strong

virtuoso highly skilled artist

virulent deadly, poisonous, infectious

visage facial expression

viscid thick, gummy

visitation a formal visit

vital necessary

vitiate spoil, ruin

vitreous glassy

vitriolic scathing

vituperative abusive, critical language

vivacious lively, high-spirited

vivid lifelike, clear

vivisection experimentation on animals, dissection

vocation occupation

vociferous adamant, clamoring

vogue fashion, chic

volant agile

volatile unstable, precarious

volition free will

voluble talkative

voluminous bulky, extensive

voracious hungry

votary fan, aficionado

vouchsafe confer, bestow

vulgarity obscenity

vulnerable susceptible

vulpine fox-like, cunning

W

wager bet
waggish playful
waive forego
wallow indulge
wan pale, pallid, listless
wane dissipate, wither
want need, poverty, lack of
wanton lewd, abandoned, gratuitous
warrant justification
wary guarded, cautious
wastrel spendthrift
waylay ambush, accost
wean remove from nursing, break a habit
weir dam
welter confusion, hodgepodge
wheedle to coax with flattery
whet stimulate
whiffle vacillate
whimsical capricious, playful
wield exercise control
willful deliberate, wanton
wily shrewd, crafty
wince cringe
windfall bonus, boon
winnow separate
winsome charmingly innocent
wistful sad yearning, melancholy

wither shrivel
wizened shriveled
woe anguish, despair
wont custom, habit
woo court, seek favor
wraith ghost
wrath anger, fury
wreak to inflict something violent
wrest snatch
wretched miserable
writ summons, court order
writhe contort, thrash about
wry twisted, ironic sense of humor

X

xenophillic attraction to strangers
xenophobia fear of foreigners
xylophone musical percussion instrument

Y

yarn story, tale
yearn desire strongly
yen desire, yearning
yore long ago
Young Turks reformers

Z

zeal earnestness, passion

zealot fanatic

zenith summit

zephyr gentle breeze

Quiz 37 (Sentence Completions)

Complete each sentence with the best available word. Answers are on page 102.

1. Though most explicitly sexist words have been replaced by gender-neutral terms, sexism thrives in the _____ of many words.

   (A) indistinctness
   (B) similitude
   (C) loquacity
   (D) implications
   (E) obscurity

2. The aspiring candidate's performance in the debate all but _____ any hope he may have had of winning the election.

   (A) nullifies
   (B) encourages
   (C) guarantees
   (D) accentuates
   (E) contains

3. She is the most _____ person I have ever met, seemingly with an endless reserve of energy.

   (A) jejune
   (B) vivacious
   (C) solicitous
   (D) impudent
   (E) indolent

4. Despite all its _____, a stint in the diplomatic core is invariably an uplifting experience.

   (A) merits
   (B) compensation
   (C) effectiveness
   (D) rigors
   (E) mediocrity

5. Robert Williams' style of writing has an air of _____: just when you think the story line is predictable, he suddenly takes a different direction. Although this is often the mark of a beginner, Williams pulls it off masterfully.

   (A) ineptness
   (B) indignation
   (C) reserve
   (D) jollity
   (E) capriciousness

6. Though a small man, J. Edgar Hoover appeared to be much larger behind his desk; for, having skillfully designed his office, he was _____ by the perspective.

   (A) augmented
   (B) comforted
   (C) apprehended
   (D) lessened
   (E) disconcerted

7. Existentialism can be used to rationalize evil: if one does not like the rules of society and has no conscience, he may use existentialism as a means of _____ a set of beliefs that are advantageous to him but injurious to others.

   (A) thwarting
   (B) proving
   (C) promoting
   (D) justifying
   (E) impugning

8. These categories amply point out the fundamental desire that people have to express themselves and the cleverness they display in that expression; who would have believed that the drab, mundane DMV would become the _____ such creativity?

   (A) catalyst for
   (B) inhibitor of
   (C) disabler of
   (D) referee of
   (E) censor of

9. This argues well that Erikson exercised less free will than Warner; for even though Erikson was aware that he was misdirected, he was still unable to _____ free will.

   (A) defer
   (B) facilitate
   (C) proscribe
   (D) prevent
   (E) exert

10. Man has no choice but to seek truth, he is made uncomfortable and frustrated without truth—thus, the quest for truth is part of what makes us _____ .

    (A) noble
    (B) different
    (C) human
    (D) intelligent
    (E) aggressive

Answers to Quizzes

Quiz 1	Quiz 2	Quiz 3	Quiz 4	Quiz 5	Quiz 6	Quiz 7	Quiz 8
1. I	1. E	1. B	1. A	1. J	1. E	1. A	1. E
2. G	2. B	2. F	2. C	2. I	2. A	2. J	2. B
3. E	3. D	3. G	3. E	3. H	3. C	3. I	3. D
4. F	4. A	4. H	4. A	4. G	4. E	4. E	4. E
5. C	5. E	5. E	5. A	5. F	5. D	5. D	5. E
6. D	6. A	6. A	6. E	6. E	6. A	6. G	6. E
7. B	7. C	7. C	7. A	7. D	7. C	7. F	7. C
8. J	8. D	8. D	8. B	8. C	8. B	8. H	8. E
9. A	9. B	9. J	9. C	9. B	9. E	9. C	9. D
10. H	10. A	10. I	10. C	10. A	10. B	10. B	10. C

Quiz 9	Quiz 10	Quiz 11	Quiz 12	Quiz 13	Quiz 14	Quiz 15	Quiz 16
1. B	1. B	1. D	1. A	1. B	1. D	1. J	1. B
2. A	2. C	2. J	2. B	2. A	2. E	2. I	2. E
3. D	3. D	3. I	3. D	3. J	3. B	3. H	3. A
4. C	4. A	4. A	4. D	4. H	4. B	4. G	4. E
5. F	5. E	5. F	5. A	5. I	5. C	5. F	5. D
6. E	6. B	6. E	6. B	6. G	6. D	6. E	6. A
7. H	7. C	7. H	7. C	7. F	7. C	7. D	7. E
8. G	8. A	8. G	8. A	8. D	8. C	8. C	8. B
9. J	9. B	9. C	9. D	9. E	9. B	9. B	9. D
10. I	10. E	10. B	10. B	10. C	10. C	10. A	10. C

Quiz 17	Quiz 18	Quiz 19	Quiz 20	Quiz 21	Quiz 22	Quiz 23	Quiz 24
1. E	1. D	1. D	1. A	1. J	1. E	1. F	1. A
2. F	2. B	2. E	2. D	2. F	2. E	2. G	2. E
3. G	3. E	3. F	3. D	3. I	3. C	3. H	3. E
4. H	4. C	4. A	4. C	4. H	4. B	4. I	4. A
5. A	5. A	5. B	5. B	5. G	5. E	5. J	5. A
6. B	6. B	6. C	6. A	6. B	6. E	6. A	6. D
7. C	7. E	7. G	7. C	7. E	7. A	7. B	7. D
8. D	8. A	8. J	8. B	8. D	8. C	8. C	8. D
9. I	9. A	9. I	9. C	9. C	9. D	9. D	9. B
10. J	10. E	10. H	10. E	10. A	10. C	10. E	10. E

Quiz 25	Quiz 26	Quiz 27	Quiz 28	Quiz 29	Quiz 30	Quiz 31	Quiz 32
1. H	1. C	1. B	1. A	1. J	1. E	1. I	1. E
2. I	2. B	2. A	2. D	2. I	2. B	2. C	2. B
3. J	3. E	3. E	3. E	3. H	3. E	3. B	3. D
4. D	4. A	4. J	4. E	4. G	4. B	4. J	4. E
5. E	5. D	5. C	5. B	5. F	5. C	5. G	5. D
6. G	6. E	6. I	6. C	6. E	6. D	6. H	6. B
7. F	7. B	7. H	7. A	7. D	7. C	7. E	7. D
8. A	8. E	8. G	8. C	8. C	8. E	8. F	8. A
9. B	9. C	9. F	9. C	9. B	9. D	9. A	9. D
10. C	10. A	10. D	10. D	10. A	10. A	10. D	10. E

Quiz 33	Quiz 34	Quiz 35	Quiz 36	Quiz 37
1. C	1. J	1. F	1. D	1. D
2. D	2. I	2. G	2. J	2. A
3. A	3. H	3. D	3. G	3. B
4. B	4. G	4. C	4. A	4. D
5. G	5. F	5. J	5. I	5. E
6. H	6. E	6. A	6. H	6. A
7. E	7. D	7. B	7. C	7. D
8. F	8. C	8. I	8. F	8. A
9. J	9. B	9. H	9. E	9. E
10. I	10. A	10. E	10. B	10. C

Techniques for Learning New Vocabulary

Put The Definition In Your Own Words

The first technique for learning new words is to put the definition in your own words. It is best to try to condense the definition to only one or two words; this will make it easier to remember. You will find simple one or two word definitions provided for you in the list of 4000 essential words in this book. You may be even more likely to remember these, however, if you put the definitions in your own words. For example, take the word

Heinous

The definition of *heinous* is "abominable, vile." However, you may find it much easier to remember by the word

Horrible

Often the dictionary definition of a word can be simplified by condensing the definition into one word. Take, for example, the word

Expiate

The dictionary definition is "to put an end to; to extinguish guilt, to make amends for." This definition may be summed up by one word

Atone

Putting definitions in your own words makes them more familiar and therefore easier to remember.

WHEN YOU DON'T KNOW THE WORD

As we mentioned, you can't possibly memorize the whole dictionary, and, while you can learn the words in a list of words that occur most frequently on the GRE, there will inevitably still be some that you do not know. Don't be discouraged. Again, there are some very effective techniques that can be applied when a word does not look familiar to you.

Put The Word In Context

In our daily speech, we combine words into phrases and sentences; rarely do we use a word by itself. This can cause words that we have little trouble understanding in sentences to suddenly appear unfamiliar when we view them in isolation. For example, take the word

Whet

Most people don't recognize it in isolation. Yet, most people understand it in the following phrase:

To whet your appetite

Whet means to "stimulate."

If you don't recognize the meaning of a word, think of a phrase in which you have heard it used.

For another example, take the word

Hallow

In isolation, it may seem unfamiliar to you. However, you probably understand its use in the phrase

The hallowed halls of academia

Hallow means "to make sacred, to honor."

Problem Set A:

For the following antonyms think of a common phrase in which the capitalized word is used.

Directions: For the following problems, choose the word most opposite in meaning to the capitalized word.

1. GRATUITOUS:
(A) voluntary (B) arduous (C) solicitous (D) righteous (E) befitting

2. FALLOW:
(A) fatuous (B) productive (C) bountiful (D) pertinacious
(E) opprobrious

3. METTLE:
(A) ad hoc (B) perdition (C) woe (D) trepidation (E) apathy

4. SAVANT:
(A) dolt (B) sage (C) attaché (D) apropos comment
(E) state of confusion

5. RIFE:
(A) multitudinous (B) blemished (C) sturdy (D) counterfeit (E) sparse

6. ABRIDGE:
(A) distend (B) assail (C) unfetter (D) enfeeble (E) prove

7. PRODIGAL:
(A) bountiful (B) dependent (C) provident (D) superfluous (E) profligate

8. REQUIEM:
(A) humility (B) prerequisite (C) resolution (D) reign (E) hiatus

9. METE:
(A) indict (B) convoke (C) hamper (D) disseminate (E) deviate

10. SEVERANCE:
(A) continuation (B) dichotomy (C) astringency (D) disclosure
(E) remonstrance

Change The Word Into A More Common Form

Most words are built from other words. Although you may not know a given word, you may spot the root word from which it is derived and thereby deduce the meaning of the original word.

Example 1: PERTURBATION: (A) impotence (B) obstruction
 (C) prediction (D) equanimity (E) chivalry

You may not know how to pronounce PERTURBATION let alone know what it means. However, changing its ending yields the more common form of the word "perturbed," which means "upset, agitated." The opposite of upset is calm, which is exactly what EQUANIMITY means. The answer is (D).

Example 2: TEMPESTUOUS: (A) prodigal (B) reticent (C) serene (D) phenomenal (E) accountable

TEMPESTUOUS is a hard word. However, if we drop the ending "stuous" and add the letter "r" we get the common word "temper." The opposite of having a temper is being calm or SERENE. The answer is (C).

Problem Set B:

For each of the following problems change the capitalized word into a more common form of the word and then find its antonym.

1. HYPOCRITICAL: (A) forthright (B) judicious (C) circumspect (D) puritanical (E) unorthodox

2. VOLUMINOUS: (A) obscure (B) cantankerous (C) unsubstantial (D) tenacious (E) opprobrious

3. FANATICISM: (A) delusion (B) fascism (C) remorse (D) cynicism (E) indifference

4. INTERMINABLE: (A) finite (B) jejune (C) tranquil (D) incessant (E) imprudent

5. ORNATE: (A) Spartan (B) blemished (C) sturdy (D) counterfeit (E) temporary

6. MUTABILITY: (A) simplicity (B) apprehension (C) frailty (D) maverick (E) tenacity

7. VIRULENT: (A) benign (B) intrepid (C) malignant (D) hyperbolic (E) tentative

8. ABSTEMIOUS: (A) timely (B) immoderate (C) bellicose (D) servile (E) irreligious

9. VERBOSE: (A) subliminal (B) myopic (C) pithy (D) dauntless (E) ubiquitous

10. VISCID: (A) subtle (B) faint (C) slick (D) vicious (E) difficult

Test Words For Positive And Negative Connotations

Testing words for positive and negative connotations is a very effective technique. Surprisingly, you can often discern the meaning of a word knowing only that the word has a negative connotation.

Example 1: REPUDIATE: (A) denounce (B) deceive (C) embrace
(D) fib (E) generalize

You may not know what REPUDIATE means, but you probably sense that it has a negative connotation. Since we are looking for a word whose meaning is opposite of REPUDIATE, we eliminate any answer-choices that are also negative. Now, "denounce," "deceive," and "fib" are all, to varying degrees, negative. So, eliminate them. "Generalize" has a neutral connotation: it can be positive, negative, or neither. So, eliminate it as well. Hence, by process of elimination, the answer is (C), EMBRACE.

Example 2: NOXIOUS: (A) diffuse (B) latent (C) beneficial
(D) unique (E) unjust

NOXIOUS has a negative connotation (strongly so). Therefore, we are looking for a word with a positive connotation. Now "diffuse" means "spread out, widely scattered." Hence, it is neutral in meaning, neither positive nor negative. Thus, we eliminate it. "Latent" and "unique" are also neutral in meaning—eliminate. "Unjust" has a negative connotation—eliminate. The only word remaining, BENEFICIAL, has a strongly positive connotation and is the answer.

> **Any GRE Word That Starts With "De," "Dis," or "Anti" Will Almost Certainly Be Negative.**

Examples: Degradation, Discrepancy, Discriminating, Debase, Antipathy

> **Any GRE Word That Includes The Notion of Going up Will Almost Certainly Be Positive, and any GRE Word That Includes The Notion of Going Down Will Almost Certainly Be Negative.**

Examples (positive): Elevate, Ascendancy, Lofty

Examples (negative): Decline, Subjugate, Suborn (to encourage false witness)

Problem Set C:

Solve the following problems by checking for positive and negative connotations.

1. DERISION: (A) urgency (B) admonishment (C) uniqueness (D) diversity (E) acclaim

2. ANTIPATHY: (A) fondness (B) disagreement (C) boorishness (D) provocation (E) opprobrium

3. CAJOLE: (A) implore (B) glance at (C) belittle (D) ennoble (E) engender

4. CENSURE: (A) prevaricate (B) titillate (C) aggrandize (D) obscure (E) sanction

5. ADULATION: (A) immutability (B) reluctance (C) reflection (D) defamation (E) indifference

6. NOISOME: (A) salubrious (B) affable (C) multifarious (D) provident (E) officious

7. CONSECRATE: (A) curb (B) destroy (C) curse (D) inveigh (E) exculpate

8. ILLUSTRIOUS: (A) bellicose (B) ignoble (C) theoretical (D) esoteric (E) immaculate

9. DEIGN: (A) inveigh (B) gainsay (C) speculate (D) reject (E) laud

10. SUBTERFUGE: (A) bewilderment (B) artlessness (C) deceit (D) felicitation (E) jeopardy

Be Alert To Secondary (Often Rare) Meanings Of Words

The GRE writers often use common words but with their uncommon meanings. An example will illustrate.

Example 1: CHAMPION: (A) relinquish (B) contest (C) oppress (D) modify (E) withhold

The common meaning of CHAMPION is "winner." Its opposite would be "loser." But no answer-choice given above is synonymous with "loser." CHAMPION also means to support or fight for someone else. (Think of the phrase "to champion a cause.") Hence, the answer is (C), OPPRESS.

Problem Set D:

In solving the following problems, look for secondary meanings.

1. CURB: (A) bridle   (B) encourage   (C) reproach   (D) ameliorate   (E) perjure

2. DOCUMENT: (A) copy   (B) implement   (C) gainsay   (D) blanch   (E) rant

3. FLUID: (A) radiant   (B) smooth   (C) solid   (D) balky   (E) craggy

4. BOLT: (A) linger   (B) refrain from   (C) subdue   (D) strip   (E) transgress

5. TABLE: (A) palliate   (B) acclimate   (C) garner   (D) propound   (E) expedite

6. HARBOR: (A) provide shelter   (B) banish   (C) acquiesce   (D) extol   (E) capitulate

7. FLOWER: (A) burgeon   (B) exact   (C) blight   (D) refute   (E) stabilize

8. STEEP: (A) desiccate   (B) intensify   (C) pontificate   (D) whet   (E) hamper

9. RENT: (A) reserved   (B) restored   (C) razed   (D) busy   (E) kinetic

10. EXACT: (A) extract   (B) starve   (C) lecture   (D) menace   (E) condone

Use Your Past Knowledge / Education

Since you are studying for the GRE, you have probably completed, or almost completed, your undergraduate studies. Therefore, you have a wealth of knowledge from which to draw when it comes to examining the words that will appear on the test. In your undergraduate classes, you studied history and probably one or more foreign languages. You may have even taken a Latin class. Because the English language has "borrowed" many words from other languages, especially Latin and French, these classes give you valuable clues to the meanings of many of the words you may come across.

Example 1:   NARCISSISTIC: (A) egocentric   (B) complacent   (C) pretentious   (D) unostentatious   (E) unassertive

You may remember Narcissus from one of your literature and Greek mythology classes. One version of the story of Narcissus relates a man who falls in love with his own reflection in a pool. Because of his requited love, he dies. As a man in love with his own reflection, he portrays self-love to the ultimate degree. A man like this is pretentious. *Unostentatious* is the opposite of *pretentious*. Hence, the answer is (D), UNOSTENTATIOUS.

Example 2: VERDANT: (A) naïve   (B) seasoned   (C) ignorant   (D) amateur   (E) innocent

Recall from your Spanish class that *verde* means "green" and from your French class that *vert* means "green" as well. These words may remind you of the word *verdant*, which also means "green" and can refer to being "green" in experience or judgment. Therefore, in this example, (B), SEASONED, is the answer because it means "experienced."

Problem Set E:

Use your past knowledge and education to solve the following problems.

1. BLARNEY: (A) eloquence   (B) loquacity   (C) volubleness   (D) taciturnity   (E) efficacy

2. BRAVADO: (A) valor   (B) brevity   (C) audacity   (D) cowardice   (E) chauvinism

3. BLASÉ: (A) satiated   (B) humdrum   (C) provoked   (D) jovial   (E) robust

4. SABOTAGE: (A) subvert   (B) advocate   (C) extricate   (D) undermine   (E) emancipate

5. GRATIS: (A) unsatisfactory   (B) gratuitous   (C) baneful   (D) commensurable   (E) extravagant

6. PROTÉGÉ: (A) prodigy   (B) pedagogue   (C) liegeman   (D) prodigal   (E) imbecile

7. PEJORATIVE: (A) depreciatory   (B) candid   (C) ameliorative   (D) disparaging   (E) veracious

8. AMOROUS: (A) abhorrent   (B) congenial   (C) unadorned   (D) magnanimous   (E) menacing

9. ACQUIESCE: (A) concede   (B) bestow   (C) accede   (D) mete   (E) dissent

10. INCOGNITO: (A) recondite   (B) palpable   (C) inconspicuous   (D) occultation   (E) disguise

Points to Remember

Techniques To Learn New Words

- Put the definition in your own words
- Write down the words
- Use flashcards
- Create a word picture
- Set goals

When You Don't Know The Word

- Put the word in context
- Change the word into a more common form
- Test words for positive and negative connotation
- Watch out for eye-catchers
- Be alert to secondary (often rare) meanings of words
- Use your past education/knowledge

Tips

- If the word starts with "De," "Dis," or "Anti," the word most likely has a negative connotation.
- If the word contains the notion of going up, it will most likely have a positive connotation.
- If the word contains the notion of going down, it will most likely have a negative connotation.

Answers and Solutions to Problems

Set A	Set B	Set C	Set D	Set E
1. E	1. A	1. E	1. B	1. D
2. B	2. C	2. A	2. C	2. A
3. D	3. E	3. C	3. D	3. C
4. A	4. A	4. E	4. A	4. B
5. E	5. A	5. D	5. E	5. E
6. A	6. E	6. A	6. B	6. B
7. C	7. A	7. C	7. C	7. C
8. D	8. B	8. B	8. A	8. A
9. B	9. C	9. E	9. B	9. E
10. A	10. C	10. B	10. E	10. B

Problem Set A:

1. You may not recognize GRATUITOUS in isolation, but you probably understand it in the phrase: "Gratuitous sex and violence." GRATUITOUS means "freely given, uncalled for." The opposite is BEFITTING. The answer is (E).

2. Think of the phrase: "Fallow youth." FALLOW means idle. The opposite is PRODUCTIVE. The answer is (B).

3. Think of the phrase: "To test your mettle." (The large waves tested the surfer's mettle.) METTLE means "character, courage." The opposite is TREPIDATION, which means fear. The answer is (D).

4. Think of the description: "Idiot-savant." An idiot-savant is a person who exhibits the characteristics of both a mentally retarded person and a mental gifted person. SAVANT means "reflective thinker." The opposite is a DOLT. The answer is (A).

5. You may have heard RIFE used in the following manner: "The city is rife with crime." RIFE means "widespread, permeated." The opposite is SPARSE. The answer is (E).

6. Think of the description: "Unabridged dictionary." An unabridged dictionary is the unabbreviated version of a dictionary. Hence, ABRIDGE means "to shorten." The opposite is DISTEND: to swell or protrude. The answer is (A).

7. Think of the description: "Prodigal son." The prodigal son is the wasteful, spoiled son—a playboy. Hence, PRODIGAL means "immoderate." The opposite is PROVIDENT—frugal, careful. The answer is (C).

8. Think of the phrase: "Requiem for a heavyweight." REQUIEM means "a rest from an arduous task." The opposite is REIGN, the time spent in power or at the top. The answer is (D).

9. Think of the phrase: "to mete out justice." METE means "to dispense, to distribute." The opposite is to gather, which is the meaning of CONVOKE. The answer is (B).

10. Think of the description: "severance pay," which is the income you continue to receive after you have stopped working for a company. SEVERANCE means "the act of breaking off (or severing) a relationship." The opposite is to continue the relationship. The answer is (A).

Problem Set B:

1. HYPOCRITICAL contains the base word HYPOCRITE, one who deceives. The opposite is one who is honest and candid. The answer is (A), FORTHRIGHT.

2. Embedded in the word VOLUMINOUS is the word VOLUME. So, we are looking for a word that is related to size. The only answer related to size is UNSUBSTANTIAL. The answer is (C). (VOLUMINOUS means "large.")

3. FANATICISM contains FANATIC which in turn contains FAN. Now, at a sporting event, fans often become overenthusiastic, which is precisely the meaning of FANATIC. Thus, we are looking for a word that means unenthusiastic. That is the meaning of INDIFFERENCE. The answer is (E).

4. INTERMINABLE comes from the base word TERMINATE—to stop. Now, the prefix *in* means "not," so INTERMINABLE means "not able to stop." The only word that contains the notion of stopping or limitedness is FINITE. Hence, the answer is (A).

5. Changing the ending of ORNATE to "ment" yields the more familiar word ORNAMENT—a decoration. The opposite is undecorated. Now, the best answer-choice is SPARTAN, which means "plain or austere." The answer is (A).

6. Changing the ending of MUTABILITY from "ability" to "ate" yields the more common word MUTATE—to change. So, we're looking for a word that means "unchanging." TENACITY means "steadfastness in one's opinions." In other words, not changing one's opinion easily. The answer is (E).

7. Dropping "lent" from VIRULENT and adding "s" yields the common word VIRUS. A VIRUS is harmful, so we want a word that means harmless, which is precisely the meaning of BENIGN. The answer is (A).

8. ABSTEMIOUS comes from ABSTAIN—to refrain from doing. The opposite is to do too much. Now, IMMODERATE means "excessive, indulgent." Hence, the answer is (B).

9. VERBOSE contains the word VERB, which means "word." VERBOSE means "too many words, wordy." Now, PITHY means "well put, concise." Hence, the answer is (C).

10. You have probably never seen the word VISCID, but changing the ending yields viscous or viscosity. The viscosity of oil is a measure of the thickness or gumminess of oil. Hence, VISCID means thick or gummy, and the opposite of gummy is SLICK. The answer is (C).

Problem Set C:

1. Since DERISION starts with DE, it should be negative. So, we are looking for a positive word. "Urgency" and "admonishment" are both somewhat negative—eliminate. "Uniqueness" and "diversity" are both neutral—eliminate. Hence, by process of elimination, the answer is (E), "acclaim." DERISION means "scorn."

2. Since ANTIPATHY starts with ANTI, it is negative. "Disagreement" "boorishness," "provocation," and "opprobrium" are all negative to varying degrees. Hence, the answer is (A), "fondness." ANTIPATHY means "hatred."

3. CAJOLE has a positive connotation. "Implore," "ennoble," and "engender" are all neutral to positive, and they are all similar to CAJOLE—eliminate. "Glance at" is neutral—eliminate. Thus, by process of elimination, the answer is (C), "belittle." CAJOLE means "to encourage."

4. CENSURE is a hard word. Nonetheless, you may sense that it has a negative connotation. (It comes from the same root as does "censor.") Hence, we want a positive word. "Sanction" is the only positive word offered, and it is the answer. CENSURE means "to deplore." The answer is (E).

5. ADULATION has a positive connotation. "Immutability," "reluctance," "reflection," and "indifference" are all neutral in connotation—eliminate. Thus, by process of elimination, the answer is (D), "defamation." ADULATION means "praise, applause."

6. NOISOME is a very negative word, so we are looking for a very positive word. Now, "multifarious" is neutral: it means "diverse, many-sided." "Provident" is a positive synonym for "miserly." "Officious" is negative: it means "acting like an official, sticking your nose into other people's business." Finally, both "salubrious" and "affable" are positive, but "salubrious" (healthful) is more positive. So (A) is the answer. NOISOME means "noxious."

7. CONSECRATE (to make holy) has a positive connotation. The only negative word is "curse." The answer is (C). Note: "Destroy" is neutral, not negative: you can destroy something that is good or bad.

8. ILLUSTRIOUS has a positive connotation. Now, "bellicose" and "ignoble" are equally negative. At this point you have to guess. The answer is (B), "ignoble," which means dishonorable. ILLUSTRIOUS means "honored, renowned."

9. Since DEIGN starts with DE, it should be negative. So, we are looking for a positive word. "Inveigh" is negative; it means to rail against. Eliminate (A). "Gainsay" is also negative; it means "to contradict, to impugn." Eliminate (B). "Speculate" is neutral as is "reject," rejecting something may be wise or unwise depending on the circumstance—eliminate (C) and (D). Hence, by process of elimination, the answer is (E). DEIGN means "to condescend, to disdain." And LAUD means "to praise, to extol."

10. The prefix "sub" gives SUBTERFUGE the sense of going down. So, we expect SUBTERFUGE to have a negative connotation. Hence, we are looking for a positive word. Now, "bewilderment" is somewhat negative— eliminate. "Artlessness" (sincere, ingenuous) is positive; it may be the answer. "Deceit" is negative—eliminate. "Felicitation" (an expression of good wishes, congratulation) is also positive; it too may be the answer. "Jeopardy" is negative—eliminate. Now, SUBTERFUGE means "deceit, conspiracy." The opposite is artlessness. The answer is (B).

Problem Set D:
1. The eye-catcher is "descent." UPSHOT contains UP and the opposite of up is down, or a descent. Now, UPSHOT is a result. Whereas, an inception is the beginning of something, it does not follow anything. The answer is (E).

2. The eye-catcher is "desiccate": the opposite of "wet." However, WHET has nothing to do with water. In fact, WHET means "to stimulate." Think of the saying "To whet your appetite." The opposite of stimulating a desire or emotion is dulling or blunting it. The answer is (B).

3. Most people associate a PRODIGY with a mentally gifted child, and the opposite would be stupid. So choice (A), VACUOUS COMMENT is tempting. But this would be too easy a connection for this hard question. Now, a PRODIGY is a person with extraordinary ability or talent, but not necessarily intelligence. By extension, PRODIGY means anything extraordinary. The opposite is a COMMON OCCURRENCE. The answer is (D).

4. You may not have heard the word AMBULATORY before. But it reminds you of ambulance, which in turn reminds you of the answer-choice HOSPITALIZED. Don't be tricked: HOSPITALIZED is an eye-catcher. Now, AMBULATORY means "walking, moving about." The opposite is STATIONARY. The answer is (E).

5. One of the first associations that comes to mind with PLATITUDE is a cliché or trite comment. So, the opposite might be SINCERE COMMENT. Be careful: this analysis is too easy and too pat to be the answer to this hard problem. Now, a PLATITUDE is insincere because not much thought goes

into creating it. Hence, it is unoriginal. The opposite is original. The answer is (E), ORIGINAL COMMENT.

6. SEEMLY appears to mean "seem," and the opposite of "seem" is "imperceptible." However, "imperceptible" is an eye-catcher. The actual meaning of SEEMLY is "appropriate or proper." You may be more familiar with its antonym "unseemly." The answer is (E), UNBECOMING.

Problem Set E:

1. Since all the answer-choices are verbs, CURB cannot mean the sidewalk you park your car next to. As a verb, CURB means "to restrain or stop." The opposite of stopping an activity is encouraging it. Hence, the answer is (B).

2. As a noun, DOCUMENT means "a legal or official paper." But all the answer-choices are verbs. As a verb, DOCUMENT means "to attest to, or to supply evidence." The opposite is to contradict, which is the meaning of "gainsay." The answer is (C).

3. Since all the answer-choices are adjectives, FLUID must also be an adjective. Now, as an adjective, FLUID means "moving in a continuous, smooth manner." The opposite would be moving in a hesitating manner, which is the meaning of "balky." (Think of a "balk" in the game of baseball.) The answer is (D).

4. As a verb, BOLT means "to move quickly." (The sprinters bolted out of the starting blocks.) The opposite is to linger. The answer is (A).

5. None of the answer-choices are nouns, so TABLE cannot be referring to furniture. As a verb, TABLE means "to postpone." You may have heard it used in government: "Congress tabled the bill." The opposite is to expedite. The answer is (E).

   Choice (D), "propound," is second-best. However, "expedite" is more precisely opposite because it includes the notion of speeding up the consideration of a proposal.

6. As a verb HARBOR mean means "to conceal" (to harbor a criminal). The opposite is to send away, which is the meaning of banish. The answer is (B).

7. As a verb, FLOWER means "to flourish," and the opposite is blight. The answer is (C).

8. As an adjective, STEEP means "precipitous." But as a verb, STEEP means "to saturate." Think of the phrase, "Steeped in tradition." In other words, filled with tradition. The opposite is to dry up, which is the meaning of desiccate. The answer is (A).

9. This is a hard problem. Unfortunately, the common meaning of RENT (payment) will not be tested on the GRE. As a verb, RENT means "to tear apart." The opposite is to RESTORE. The answer is (B).

10. As an adjective, EXACT means "accurate." But as a verb, EXACT means "to use authority to force payment or compliance." The opposite is to CONDONE: to allow or forgive. The answer is (E).

Problem Set F:

1. Legend has it that if you kiss a magical stone in Blarney, Ireland, you will be given the gift of flattering speech, or eloquence. The opposite of BLARNEY, then, is TACITURNITY, which means silence or reticence. The answer is (D).

2. BRAVADO comes from Old Spanish *bravada* or French *bravade*. Someone who shows bravado shows a pretense of bravery. The opposite of a pretense of bravery is true bravery, which is the meaning of VALOR. The answer is (A).

3. BLASÉ is a French word, which means to sicken. The meaning of the word is to become world-weary or apathetic to pleasure or excitement. PROVOKED means to arouse or provide stimulation. The answer is (C).

4. SABOTAGE, a French word, means treason or destruction. To ADVOCATE means to support. The answer is (B).

5. GRATIS comes from Latin, and you may also recognize it from the French word *gratuit*. It means free of charge. EXTRAVAGANT is the opposite of gratis. The answer is (E).

6. PROTÉGÉ comes from the French word *protéger*, which means to protect. A protégé is protected by a mentor, which is the opposite of protégé. One type of mentor is a teacher or PEDAGOGUE. The answer is (B).

7. PEJORATIVE comes from the French word *péjoratif*, which means to worsen. The opposite is ameliorative. The answer is (C).

8. You've heard the saying "Love in any language." The meaning of AMOROUS clearly relates to love. Recall from your undergraduate classes that love in French is *amour*, in Spanish *amor*, and in Italian *amore*. The opposite of love is hate. ABHORRENT means characteristic of loathing. The answer is (A).

9. ACQUIESCE comes from the French word *acquiescer*, which means to consent or agree passively. The opposite of acquiesce is DISSENT. The answer is (E).

10. INCOGNITO is Italian and means unknown or disguised. The word has its roots in the Latin word *cognoscere*, which means to get to know. Add the prefix *in-*, which means "not." You may also remember the Spanish word *conocer* or the French word *connaître*, both of which mean "to know." The opposite of incognito is PALPABLE. The answer is (B).

Word Analysis

Word analysis (etymology) is the process of separating a word into its parts and then using the meanings of those parts to deduce the meaning of the original word. Take, for example, the word INTERMINABLE. It is made up of three parts: a prefix IN (not), a root TERMIN (stop), and a suffix ABLE (can do). Therefore, by word analysis, INTERMINABLE means "not able to stop." This is not the literal meaning of INTERMINABLE (endless), but it is close enough. For another example, consider the word RETROSPECT. It is made up of the prefix RETRO (back) and the root SPECT (to look). Hence, RETROSPECT means "to look back (in time), to contemplate."

Word analysis is very effective in decoding the meaning of words. However, you must be careful in its application since words do not always have the same meaning as the sum of the meanings of their parts. In fact, on occasion words can have the opposite meaning of their parts. For example, by word analysis the word AWFUL should mean "full of awe," or awe-inspiring. But over the years, it has come to mean just the opposite—terrible. In spite of the shortcomings, word analysis gives the correct meaning of a word (or at least a hint of it) far more often than not and therefore is a useful tool.

Examples:

INDEFATIGABLE

Analysis: IN (not);   DE (thoroughly);   FATIG (fatigue);   ABLE (can do)
Meaning: cannot be fatigued, tireless

CIRCUMSPECT

Analysis: CIRCUM (around);   SPECT (to look)
Meaning: to look around, that is, to be cautious

ANTIPATHY

Analysis: ANTI (against);   PATH (to feel);   Y (noun suffix)
Meaning: to feel strongly against something, to hate

OMNISCIENT

Analysis: OMNI (all);   SCI (to know);   ENT (noun suffix)
Meaning: all-knowing

Following are some of the most useful prefixes, roots, and suffixes.

Prefixes

1.	**ab**	from	aberration
2.	**ad**—also **ac, af, ag, al, an, ap, ar, as, at**	to	adequate
3.	**ambi**	both	ambidextrous
4.	**an**—also **a**	without	anarchy
5.	**anti**	against	antipathetic
6.	**ante**	before	antecedent
7.	**be**	throughout	belie
8.	**bi**	two	bilateral
9.	**cata**	down	catacomb
10.	**circum**	around	circumscribe
11.	**com**—also **con, col, cor, cog, co**	together	confluence
12.	**contra**	against	contravene
13.	**de**	down (negative)	debase
14.	**deca**	ten	decathlon
15.	**decem**	ten	decimal
16.	**di**	two	digraph
17.	**dia**	through, between	dialectic
18.	**dis**	apart (negative)	disparity
19.	**du**	two	duplicate
20.	**dys**	abnormal	dysphoria
21.	**epi**	upon	epicenter
22.	**equi**	equal	equitable
23.	**ex**	out	extricate
24.	**extra**	beyond	extraterrestrial
25.	**fore**	in front of	foreword
26.	**hemi**	half	hemisphere
27.	**hyper**	excessive	hyperbole
28.	**hypo**	too little	hypothermia

29.	**in**—also **ig, il, im, ir**	not	inefficient
30.	**in**—also **il, im, ir**	in, very	invite, inflammable
31.	**inter**	between	interloper
32.	**intro**—also **intra**	inside	introspective
33.	**kilo**	one thousand	kilogram
34.	**meta**	changing	metaphysics
35.	**micro**	small	microcosm
36.	**mili**—also **milli**	one thousand	millipede
37.	**mis**	bad, hate	misanthrope
38.	**mono**	one	monopoly
39.	**multi**	many	multifarious
40.	**neo**	new	neophyte
41.	**nil**—also **nihil**	nothing	nihilism
42.	**non**	not	nonentity
43.	**ob**—also **oc, of, op**	against	obstinate
44.	**pan**	all	panegyric
45.	**para**	beside	paranormal
46.	**per**	throughout	permeate
47.	**peri**	around	periscope
48.	**poly**	many	polyglot
49.	**post**	after	posterity
50.	**pre**	before	predecessor
51.	**prim**	first	primitive
52.	**pro**	forward	procession
53.	**quad**	four	quadruple
54.	**re**	again	reiterate
55.	**retro**	backward	retrograde
56.	**semi**	half	semiliterate
57.	**sub**—also **suc, suf, sug, sup, sus**	under	succumb
58.	**super**—also **supra**	above	superannuated
59.	**syn**—also **sym, syl**	together	synthesis
60.	**trans**	across	transgression
61.	**un**	not	unkempt

| 62. **uni** | one | unique |

Roots

Root	Meaning	Example
1. **ac**	bitter, sharp	acrid
2. **agog**	leader	demagogue
3. **agri**—also **agrari**	field	agriculture
4. **ali**	other	alienate
5. **alt**	high	altostratus
6. **alter**	other	alternative
7. **am**	love	amiable
8. **anim**	soul	animadversion
9. **anthrop**	man, people	anthropology
10. **arch**	ruler	monarch
11. **aud**	hear	auditory
12. **auto**	self	autocracy
13. **belli**	war	bellicose
14. **ben**	good	benevolence
15. **biblio**	book	bibliophile
16. **bio**	life	biosphere
17. **cap**	take	caprice
18. **capit**	head	capitulate
19. **carn**	flesh	incarnate
20. **ced**	go	accede
21. **celer**	swift	accelerate
22. **cent**	one hundred	centurion
23. **chron**	time	chronology
24. **cide**	cut, kill	fratricide
25. **cit**	to call	recite
26. **civ**	citizen	civility
27. **cord**	heart	cordial
28. **corp**	body	corporeal

29. **cosm**	universe	cosmopolitan
30. **crat**	power	plutocrat
31. **cred**	belief	incredulous
32. **cur**	to care	curable
33. **deb**	debt	debit
34. **dem**	people	demagogue
35. **dic**	to say	Dictaphone
36. **doc**	to teach	doctorate
37. **dynam**	power	dynamism
38. **ego**	I	egocentric
39. **err**	to wander	errant
40. **eu**	good	euphemism
41. **fac**—also **fic, fec, fect**	to make	affectation
42. **fall**	false	infallible
43. **fer**	to carry	fertile
44. **fid**	faith	confidence
45. **fin**	end	finish
46. **fort**	strong	fortitude
47. **gen**	race, group	genocide
48. **geo**	earth	geology
49. **germ**	vital part	germane
50. **gest**	carry	gesticulate
51. **gnosi**	know	prognosis
52. **grad**—also **gress**	step	transgress
53. **graph**	writing	calligraphy
54. **grav**	heavy	gravitate
55. **greg**	crowd	egregious
56. **habit**	to have, live	habituate
57. **hema**—also **hemo**	blood	hemorrhage
58. **hetero**	different	heterogeneous
59. **homo**	same	homogenized

60. **hum**	earth, man	humble
61. **jac**—also **jec**	throw	interjection
62. **jud**	judge	judicious
63. **junct**—also **join**	combine	disjunctive
64. **jus**—also **jur**	law, to swear	adjure
65. **leg**	law	legislator
66. **liber**	free	libertine
67. **lic**	permit	illicit
68. **loc**	place	locomotion
69. **log**	word	logic
70. **loqu**	speak	soliloquy
71. **macro**	large	macrobiotics
72. **magn**	large	magnanimous
73. **mal**	bad	malevolent
74. **manu**	by hand	manuscript
75. **matr**	mother	matriarch
76. **medi**	middle	medieval
77. **meter**	measure	perimeter
78. **mit**—also **miss**	send	missive
79. **morph**	form, structure	anthropomorphic
80. **mut**	change	immutable
81. **nat**—also **nasc**	born	nascent
82. **neg**	deny	renegade
83. **nomen**	name	nominal
84. **nov**	new	innovative
85. **omni**	all	omniscient
86. **oper**—also **opus**	work	operative
87. **pac**—also **plais**	please	complaisant
88. **pater**—also **patr**	father	expatriate
89. **path**	disease, feeling	pathos
90. **ped**—also **pod**	foot	pedestal

91.	**pel**—also **puls**	push	impulsive
92.	**pen**	hang	appendix
93.	**phil**	love	philanthropic
94.	**pict**	paint	depict
95.	**poli**	city	metropolis
96.	**port**	carry	deportment
97.	**pos**—also **pon**	to place	posit
98.	**pot**	power	potentate
99.	**put**	think	computer
100.	**rect**—also **reg**	straight	rectitude
101.	**ridi**—also **risi**	laughter	derision
102.	**rog**	beg	interrogate
103.	**rupt**	break	interruption
104.	**sanct**	holy	sanctimonious
105.	**sangui**	blood	sanguinary
106.	**sat**	enough	satiate
107.	**sci**	know	conscience
108.	**scrib**—also **script**	to write	circumscribe
109.	**sequ**—also **secu**	follow	sequence
110.	**simil**—also **simul**	resembling	simile
111.	**solv**—also **solut**	loosen	absolve
112.	**soph**	wisdom	unsophisticated
113.	**spec**	look	circumspect
114.	**spir**	breathe	aspire
115.	**strict**—also **string**	bind	astringent
116.	**stru**	build	construe
117.	**tact**—also **tang, tig**	touch	intangible
118.	**techni**	skill	technique
119.	**tempor**	time	temporal
120.	**ten**	hold	tenacious
121.	**term**	end	interminable

122. **terr**	earth	extraterrestrial
123. **test**	to witness	testimony
124. **the**	god	theocracy
125. **therm**	heat	thermodynamics
126. **tom**	cut	epitome
127. **tort**—also **tors**	twist	distortion
128. **tract**	draw, pull	abstract
129. **trib**	bestow	attribute
130. **trud**—also **trus**	push	protrude
131. **tuit**—also **tut**	teach	intuitive
132. **ultima**	last	penultimate
133. **ultra**	beyond	ultraviolet
134. **urb**	city	urbane
135. **vac**	empty	vacuous
136. **val**	strength, valor	valediction
137. **ven**	come	adventure
138. **ver**	true	veracity
139. **verb**	word	verbose
140. **vest**	clothe	travesty
141. **vic**	change	vicissitude
142. **vit**—also **viv**	alive	vivacious
143. **voc**	voice	vociferous
144. **vol**	wish	volition

Suffixes determine the part of speech a word belongs to. They are not as useful for determining a word's meaning as are roots and prefixes. Nevertheless, there are a few that are helpful.

Suffixes

Suffix	Meaning	Example
1. **able**—also **ible**	capable of	legible
2. **acy**	state of	celibacy
3. **ant**	full of	luxuriant
4. **ate**	to make	consecrate
5. **er, or**	one who	censor
6. **fic**	making	traffic
7. **ism**	belief	monotheism
8. **ist**	one who	fascist
9. **ize**	to make	victimize
10. **oid**	like	steroid
11. **ology**	study of	biology
12. **ose**	full of	verbose
13. **ous**	full of	fatuous
14. **tude**	state of	rectitude
15. **ure**	state of, act	primogeniture

Exercise:

Analyze and define the following words.

Example: **RETROGRADE**
Analysis: retro (backward); grade (step)
Meaning: to step backward, to regress

1. **CIRCUMNAVIGATE**
   Analysis:
   Meaning:
2. **MISANTHROPE**
   Analysis:
   Meaning:
3. **ANARCHY**
   Analysis:
   Meaning:
4. **AUTOBIOGRAPHY**
   Analysis:
   Meaning:
5. **INCREDULOUS**
   Analysis:
   Meaning:
6. **EGOCENTRIC**
   Analysis:
   Meaning:
7. **INFALLIBLE**
   Analysis:
   Meaning:
8. **AMORAL**
   Analysis:
   Meaning:
9. **INFIDEL**
   Analysis:
   Meaning:
10. **NONENTITY**
    Analysis:
    Meaning:
11. **CORPULENT**
    Analysis:
    Meaning:
12. **IRREPARABLE**
    Analysis:
    Meaning:

13. **INTROSPECTIVE**
    Analysis:
    Meaning:

14. **IMMORTALITY**
    Analysis:
    Meaning:

15. **BENEFACTOR**
    Analysis:
    Meaning:

16. **DEGRADATION**
    Analysis:
    Meaning:

17. **DISPASSIONATE**
    Analysis:
    Meaning:

18. **APATHETIC**
    Analysis:
    Meaning:

Solutions to Exercise

1. **CIRCUMNAVIGATE**
   Analysis: CIRCUM (around); NAV (to sail); ATE (verb suffix)
   Meaning: To sail around the world.

2. **MISANTHROPE**
   Analysis: MIS (bad, hate); ANTHROP (man)
   Meaning: One who hates all mankind.

3. **ANARCHY**
   Analysis: AN (without); ARCH (ruler); Y (noun suffix)
   Meaning: Without rule, chaos.

4. **AUTOBIOGRAPHY**
   Analysis: AUTO (self); BIO (life); GRAPH (to write); Y (noun suffix)
   Meaning: One's written life story.

5. **INCREDULOUS**
   Analysis: IN (not); CRED (belief); OUS (adjective suffix)
   Meaning: Doubtful, unbelieving.

6. **EGOCENTRIC**
   Analysis: EGO (self); CENTR (center); IC (adjective suffix)
   Meaning: Self-centered.

7. **INFALLIBLE**
   Analysis: IN (not); FALL (false); IBLE (adjective suffix)
   Meaning: Certain, cannot fail.

8. **AMORAL**
Analysis: A (without);   MORAL (ethical)
Meaning: Without morals.

Note: AMORAL does not mean immoral; rather it means neither right nor wrong. Consider the following example: Little Susie, who does not realize that it is wrong to hit other people, hits little Bobby. She has committed an AMORAL act. However, if her mother explains to Susie that it is wrong to hit other people and she understands it but still hits Bobby, then she has committed an *immoral* act.

9. **INFIDEL**
Analysis: IN (not);   FID (belief)
Meaning: One who does not believe (of religion).

10. **NONENTITY**
Analysis: NON (not);   ENTITY (thing)
Meaning: A person of no significance.

11. **CORPULENT**
Analysis: CORP (body);   LENT (adjective suffix)
Meaning: Obese.

12. **IRREPARABLE**
Analysis: IR (not);   REPAR (to repair);   ABLE (can do)
Meaning: Something that cannot be repaired; a wrong so egregious it cannot be righted.

13. **INTROSPECTIVE**
Analysis: INTRO (within);   SPECT (to look);   IVE (adjective suffix)
Meaning: To look inward, to analyze oneself.

14. **IMMORTALITY**
Analysis: IM (not);   MORTAL (subject to death);   ITY (noun ending)
Meaning: Cannot die, will live forever.

15. **BENEFACTOR**
Analysis: BENE (good);   FACT (to do);   OR (noun suffix [one who])
Meaning: One who does a good deed, a patron.

16. **DEGRADATION**
Analysis: DE (down—negative);   GRADE (step);   TION (noun suffix)
Meaning: The act of lowering someone socially or humiliating them.

17. **DISPASSIONATE**
Analysis: DIS (away—negative);   PASS (to feel)
Meaning: Devoid of personal feeling, impartial.

18. **APATHETIC**
Analysis: A (without);   PATH (to feel); IC (adjective ending)
Meaning: Without feeling; to be uninterested. (The apathetic voters.)

Text Completions

The sentence completions used to form the most straightforward part of the test, and most students did well on them. However, with the new GRE format, ETS has decided to change the name to "text completions" and make their structure a little more complicated.

Formerly, sentences contained one or two blanks with five multiple choice answers, no matter how many blanks in the question. For example, a two-blank question used to look something like this:

> The plane had been redesigned so many times before it reached the assembly line that its _____ conception was no longer _____.
>
> (A) appropriate .. visible
> (B) dilapidated .. relevant
> (C) original .. recognizable
> (D) initial .. understandable
> (E) promised .. viable

This format makes answering the question easier, because if, for example, you weren't sure of the answer to the first blank but were confident about the second blank, you could use process of elimination to narrow down your answer choices.

Now, questions come from passages from one to five sentences long, contain anywhere from one to three blanks, and each blank has its own set of three to five multiple choice answers (five if it is a single-blank question; three if it is a multiple blank question). Answer one of the blanks wrong, and you get the entire question wrong. Yes, the stakes are high. Use the following steps, however, to master these new question types, and show those tricky GRE question writers what you're made of!

Before You Look at The Answer-Choices, Think of a Word That "Fits" The Sentence

Don't worry about coming up with a fancy or erudite word for the blank. As a matter of fact, you can make up your own word, as long as you know what it means. Then, go through the answer choices and eliminate ones that don't match your word. If none of them match your word, revisit the sentence to make sure you've understood it.

Example :

Crestfallen by having done poorly on the GRE, Susan began to question her abilities. Her self-confidence was _____ .

| appeased |
| destroyed |
| placated |
| elevated |
| sustained |

If somebody is crestfallen (despairing) and has begun to question herself, then her self-confidence would be "shot." "Appeased," "placated," "elevated," and "sustained" don't mean shot, but "destroyed" certainly does. Hence, the answer is "destroyed."

Be Alert to Transitional Words

Transitional words tell you what is coming up. They indicate that the author is now going to either draw a contrast with or support something stated previously. Recognizing these transitional words is essential for understanding the sentence or sentences.

Contrast Indicators

To contrast two things is to point out how they differ. In this type of sentence completion problem, we look for a word that has the opposite meaning (an antonym) of some key word or phrase in the sentence. Following are some of the most common contrast indicators:

BUT	YET
DESPITE	ALTHOUGH
HOWEVER	NEVERTHELESS
WHEREAS	IN CONTRAST
WHILE	THOUGH
RATHER	

Example :

Although the warring parties had settled a number of disputes, past experience made them _____ to express optimism that the talks would be a success.

| rash |
| ambivalent |
| scornful |
| overjoyed |
| reticent |

"Although" sets up a contrast between what has occurred—success on some issues—and what can be expected to occur—success for the whole talks. Hence, the parties are *reluctant* to express optimism. The common word "reluctant" is not offered as an answer-choice, but a synonym—reticent—is.

Example :
Rather than increasing its security by developing nuclear weapons, a nascent nuclear power is viewed as a _____ by its enemies.

| benefactor |
| protector |
| target |
| patron |
| non entity |

The phrase "rather than" sets up a contrast between what a country hopes to achieve by developing nuclear weapons (increased security) and what it actually achieves (becoming a target). The answer is "target."

Support Indicators

Supporting words support or further explain what has already been said. These words often introduce synonyms for words elsewhere in the sentence. Following are some common supporting words:

AND	ALSO
FURTHERMORE	LIKEWISE
IN ADDITION	FOR
INDEED	SIMILARLY
ç	

Example :
Davis is an opprobrious and _____ speaker, equally caustic toward friend or foe—a true curmudgeon.

| lofty |
| vituperative |
| unstinting |
| retiring |
| laudatory |

"And" in the sentence indicates that the missing adjective is similar in meaning to "opprobrious," which is very negative. Now, *vituperative*—the only negative word—means "abusive."

Example:

The belief that sanctions and tactical military strikes can turn the people of a country against a dictator is folly; indeed, as we are witnessing in the Balkans, this _____ causes the population to rally around the dictator.

| sometimes |
| rarely |
| invariably |
| never |
| occasionally |

"Indeed" in the sentence indicates that the second clause supports and emphasizes what is stated in the first clause: that sanctions and tactical military strikes will not work. Now, something that will not work will *invariably* (always) fail.

Cause And Effect Indicators

These words indicate that one thing causes another to occur. Some of the most common cause and effect indicators are

BECAUSE   **FOR**
THUS   **HENCE**
THEREFORE   **IF ___, THEN ___.**
ACCORDINGLY   **CONSEQUENTLY**
DUE TO

Example:

Because the Senate has the votes to override a presidential veto, the President has no choice but to _____.

| object |
| abdicate |
| abstain |
| capitulate |
| compromise |

Since the Senate has the votes to pass the bill or motion, the President would be wise to *compromise* and make the best of the situation.

Apposition

This rather advanced grammatical structure is very common on the GRE. (Don't confuse "apposition" with "opposition": they have opposite meanings.)

Words or phrases in apposition are placed next to each other, and the second word or phrase defines, clarifies, or gives evidence to the first word or phrase. The second word or phrase will be set off from the first by a comma, semicolon, hyphen, or parentheses.

HINT: If a comma is not followed by a linking word—such as *and, for, yet*—then the following phrase is probably appositional.

Identifying an appositional structure can greatly simplify a text completion problem, since the appositional word, phrase, or clause will define the missing word.

Example:

His novels are _____; he uses a long circumlocution when a direct coupling of a simple subject and verb would be best.

| prolix |
| pedestrian |
| succinct |
| vapid |
| risqué |

The sentence has no linking words (such as *because, although*, etc.). Hence, the phrase following the semicolon is in apposition to the missing word—it defines or further clarifies the missing word. Now, writing filled with circumlocutions is aptly described as "wordy" or *prolix*.

Example:

Robert Williams' style of writing has an air of _____: just when you think the story line is predictable, he suddenly takes a different direction. Although this is often the mark of a beginner, Williams pulls it off masterfully.

| ineptness |
| indignation |
| reserve |
| jollity |
| capriciousness |

There is no connecting word following the colon. Hence, the description, "*just when you think the story line is predictable, he suddenly takes a different direction*," defines the missing word. Now, something that is unpredictable because it's continually changing direction is capricious. Thus, the answer is "capriciousness."

A Note on Multiple Blank Questions

So far, we have applied the strategies discussed only to single blank questions. For questions with multiple blanks, these strategies will work as well.

However, once you have determined what you believe to be the correct answer for each blank, you will need to re-read the entire passage with each answer choice you have selected.

Sometimes, the answer to one blank affects the answer to another blank. In these instances, it may be best to answer the blanks out of order. Identify any blanks that do not seem dependent on the others, and answer this one first. Then, reread the entire passage with that blank filled in to answer the other blanks.

It is essential, however, for you to check your work on multiple blank questions. Re-read the entire sentence to ensure it makes sense before you submit your answer.

Example:

In Socrates' famous allegory of the cave, he (1) _____ the reality of the physical world, claiming instead that truth is to be found in the (2) _____ world. In the allegory, cavemen sit and stare at shadows, believing the shadows to be reality, but only a philosopher can climb out of the cave to reach heights where one can observe true and perfect forms. Thus, enlightened men are (3) _____ to guide the unenlightened.

Blank 1	Blank 2	Blank 3
asserts	metaphysical	obligated
renounces	sensual	inept
enumerates	political	provoked

The first two blanks are very interrelated. The transitional word "instead" sets up a contradiction that is essential for both blanks. Focus on the phrase *"claiming instead that truth is to be found..."* In other words, truth is *not* to be found in the physical world. So, Socrates *renounces* the reality of the physical world. Re-read the first sentence now with "renounces" in the first blank.

The second blank is tricky. We can eliminate "sensual," because that is too close in meaning to "physical," and it's supposed to be opposite. There is no justification in the sentence for "political" to be the answer. M*etaphysical* is the implied answer, as evidenced by the following sentence, which describes philosophers climbing out, attaining new heights. This imagery indicates a world higher than reality.

Finally, with the first sentence completed, one can read the entire passage and determine that Socrates has a positive view of philosophers, so he would likely believe that philosophers, or enlightened men, "should" or are *obligated* to guide the unenlightened. Rereading the passage, each of the answer choices makes sense in the passage as a whole.

Let's try another example.

Example:
Political scientists seem to never settle the ongoing debate about the relative merits of various forms of government. Democracy is one of the most (1)_____ forms, spreading to more than sixty nations in the last two hundred years. However, despite its popularity, it is also (2)_____ for not offering sufficient political stability. In contrast, though oligarchies have a history of oppression, they are praised for their (3)_____; while democracies may take months to attain a majority vote to pass an urgent law, oligarchies have the power to pass it in days.

Blank 1	Blank 2	Blank 3
defunct	lauded	forbearance
prolific	equivocated	renown
culpable	disparaged	efficacy

The first blank is the easiest, as its answer is independent of the rest of the paragraph. We are now well-practiced enough in recognizing apposition to see that "spreading to more than sixty nations in the last two hundred years" clarifies or explains the first blank. If it has spread rapidly, then it is "prolific."

For the second blank, recognize the signal word "however" and the key phrase "despite its popularity." This lets us know there will be a contrast; while a positive attribute of democracy was just described, the next must be a drawback. Thus, it would be "disparaged" for not offering political stability.

The third blank uses apposition, as indicated by the semicolon following the blank. If oligarchies can pass laws in days as opposed to months, they would be lauded for their speed and effectiveness, or "efficacy."

Problem Set:

1. Because of his success as a comedian, directors were loath to consider him for _____ roles.

supporting
leading
dramatic
comedic
musical

2. The aspiring candidate's performance in the debate all but _____ any hope he may have had of winning the election.

nullifies
encourages
guarantees
accentuates
contains

3. She is the most _____ person I have ever met, seemingly with an endless reserve of energy.

jejune
vivacious
solicitous
impudent
indolent

4. In spite of the (1) _____ vista of the country, dismantled by war and its development clogged by illiteracy, locals like to (2) _____ their nationalism.

Blank 1	Blank 2
diverse	flaunt
chaotic	curb
static	conceal

5. Liharev flirts with being both a nihilist and an atheist during his life, yet he never does _____ faith in God.

affirm
lose
scorn
aver
supplicate

6. Existentialism can be used to (1) _____ evil: if one does not like the rules of society and has no conscience, he may use existentialism as a means of (2) _____ a set of beliefs that are (3) _____ to him but injurious to others.

Blank 1	Blank 2	Blank 3
rationalize	converting	adverse
thwart	impugning	asinine
condemn	justifying	advantageous

7. These categories amply point out the (1)_____ desire that people have to express themselves and the cleverness they display in that expression; who would have believed that the drab, (2) _____ DMV would become the (3) _____ such creativity?

Blank 1	Blank 2	Blank 3
acquired	mundane	inhibitor of
fundamental	incorrigible	catalyst for
platonic	inspiring	censor of

8. This argues well that Erikson exercised less free will than Warner; for even though Erikson was aware that he was misdirected, he was still unable to _____ free will.

defer
facilitate
proscribe
prevent
exert

9. Located amidst the colossal green hills, what might have otherwise been a (1)_____ airfield in (2)_____ part of the North assumed the overtones of the battlefield.

Blank 1	Blank 2
picturesque	an estranged
combatant	an exquisite
stark	a war torn

10. Though most explicitly sexist words have been replaced by gender-neutral terms, sexism thrives in the _____ of many words.

indistinctness
similitude
loquacity
implications
obscurity

11. We landed at the airport with (1)_____ notions of the country as (2)_____ country where many parents are alleged to have sold their children in exchange for food.

Blank 1	Blank 2
unwarranted	an impotent
germane	an impoverished
preconceived	an opulent

12. Man is violent; therefore, any theory of conflict resolution between nations that (1)_____ to account for this is (2)_____ flawed.

Blank 1	Blank 2
declines	inherently
consents	pejoratively
fails	manifestly

13. Ironically, the foreign affairs policies of democracies are more likely to meet with protests than similar policies of totalitarian regimes because a democracy is _____ protest; whereas in a totalitarian regime, no one is listening.

impassive to
indifferent to
imperiled by
sensitive to
inured to

14. Although the buildings and streets of this small beach town appear (1) _____, the property values are quite (2) _____.

Blank 1	Blank 2
expensive	high
dilapidated	pedestrian
refurbished	reasonable

15. Though he claimed the business was (1)_____, his irritability (2)_____ that claim.

Blank 1	Blank 2
expanding	vindicated
static	belied
sound	affirmed

16. The rules of engagement for United Nations troops stationed in Bosnia prohibit deadly force unless all _____ actions have be exhausted.

comparable
arbitrary
alternative
apropos
extraordinary

17. Despite its lofty goal—truth—many scholars maintain that law as a _____ is a highly regulated street fight.

dogma
study
profession
philosophy
lifestyle

18. Some argue that American politics have become so (1) _____ that politicians will argue merely to gain power, and the subject of debate is often (2) _____. The vigorous dispute over where to place a comma in the Republican platform, for example, was motivated not by any significant change in meaning but by a desire not to show any (3) _____ to the other side.

Blank 1	Blank 2	Blank 3
antiquated	negligible	ambivalence
polarized	exigent	deference
homogenized	convoluted	favoritism

19. The citizenry had become so (1) _____ by the president's (2) _____ that the latest financial scandal did not even make the front page of the newspapers.

Blank 1	Blank 2
jaded	indiscretions
disgusted	magnanimity
fascinated	peccadilloes

20. In these politically correct times, it has become _____ to discuss certain subjects at all.

safe
eccentric
precarious
efficacious
effortless

21. Although the stock market has experienced strong (1) _____ in the past two years, there have been short periods in which the market has (2) _____ precipitously.

Blank 1	Blank 2
sluggishness	fallen
growth	stabilized
stagnation	increased

22. Her _____ attitude toward child-rearing was complemented with plenty of love.

austere
indifferent
ambivalent
lenient
sycophantic

23. The interviewer was startled to hear the otherwise gracious author make the _____ remark: "My novels are too sophisticated for the American public."

apt
enigmatic
bombastic
vacuous
insightful

24. The judge openly associated with racist organizations; nevertheless, he showed no _____ in his decisions during his career.

favoritism
benevolence
openness
prejudice
altruism

25. The condemnatory (1) _____ of critics directed toward Steven Spielberg's latest film attests to the fact that the pretentious critics have lost sight of the purpose of movies: (2) _____.

Blank 1	Blank 2
drivel	to entertain
laud	to correct
circumlocution	to convert

26. Suicide is the outcome of man's difficulty to _____ himself in society, so he does not feel isolated.

materialize
seclude
homogenize
secure
integrate

27. It is a situation with a hard, practical edge which raises issues of life-threatening (1)_____. Therefore, it demands to be addressed with cool, clear-headed (2)_____.

Blank 1	Blank 2
evidence	pragmatism
immediacy	erudition
existence	involvement

28. The general accused the senator of naiveté for _____ that air strikes alone could stop the aggressors.

advocating
denying
obfuscating
mishandling
disallowing

29. Hundreds of citizens showed up to (1)_____ the planning commission's master plan for regional centers, claiming that adding 800,000 additional people to the metro area by the year 2020 would cause (2)_____ and gridlock.

Blank 1	Blank 2
celebrate	overcrowding
amend	bathos
protest	duplicity

30. Though _____ toward his own material needs, he was always magnanimous toward others.

neglectful
charitable
profligate
improvident
condemnatory

31. The intelligence community should not be (1)_____ for not foreseeing the fall of the Soviet Union; even Hedrick Smith, author of *The Russians*, stated in 1986 that the Soviet Union is the world's most (2)_____ society.

Blank 1	Blank 2
applauded	arbitrary
castigated	stable
engendered	conscientious

32. Although prices (1) _____ during the fuel shortage, the suppliers actually saw (2)_____ in profits.

Blank 1	Blank 2
fluctuated	a windfall
decreased	a loss
increased	a boon

33. In the 1950s, integration was (1) _____ to most Americans; now, however, most Americans accept it as (2) _____.

Blank 1	Blank 2
an anathema	sporadic
welcome	desirable
common	mandatory

34. A more admirable character would have been one who overcame his (1) _____ impulses and became good; rather than one who merely lacked the (2) _____ to be bad.

Blank 1	Blank 2
ire	serenity
compassionate	patience
evil	sophistication

35. Although World War II ended more than half a century ago, Russia and Japan still have not signed a formal peace treaty; and both countries have been (1) _____ to develop more (2) _____ relations.

Blank 1	Blank 2
reticent	controversial
inimical	hostile
obstinate	amiable

36. Some are born with a (1)_____ to commit suicide, whereas some commit suicide because they are unable to bear (2)_____ changes in their lives.

Blank 1	Blank 2
predisposition	cataclysmic
prognosis	inimical
prodigy	perpetual

37. Today, plastic has proved to be a (1)_____ to the environment; the world over, steps are being taken to ban the (2)_____ and non-recyclable material, which has silently taken over our lives.

Blank 1	Blank 2
perquisite	non-ecofriendly
menace	ominous
boon	cacophonous

38. Despite its (1) _____ and safety in treating some of the most incapacitating forms of depression and anxiety, it has not been widely (2) _____.

Blank 1	Blank 2
usefulness	renounced
ineffectuality	accepted
potency	commenced

39. Despite her age, she has a silly and _____ sense of humor.

mature
trivial
ambiguous
asinine
youthful

40. There are different and (1) _____ versions about what happened in the city, but one thing is certain: it a dastardly act that must be condemned (2) _____.

Blank 1	Blank 2
complementary	commensurately
falsified	unequivocally
conflicting	promptly

41. By (1)_____ celebrities from the sports, entertainment, or business arenas, the show narrates the stories of the (2)_____ newsmakers from all walks of life.

Blank 1	Blank 2
narrating	influential
profiling	ordinary
parading	pedestrian

42. Behind their strange appearance and (1)_____ for carrion, which has long singled them out for fear and loathing, hyenas present a (2)_____ society in which females dominate.

Blank 1	Blank 2
penchant	realistic
aversion	matriarchal
chary	monarchal

43. At the cutting edge of research, scientists are developing new sunscreens of both _____ and internal varieties.

polar
topical
territorial
atmospheric
regional

44. Although the AIDS epidemic is in the limelight, there is a silent killer (1)_____ through India, killing more people than AIDS itself. The (2)_____ is that, unlike AIDS, this disease is easily cured.

Blank 1	Blank 2
rampaging	conundrum
digressing	conflict
alleviating	irony

45. Knowing that she was overshadowed by many other actors, Julianne recognized that she was indulging in a bit of _____ when she wondered whether Michael was the greatest living actor.

| irony |
| overemphasis |
| understatement |
| hyperbole |
| injustice |

46. Their courage is only _____; a small show of strength is enough to call their bluff.

| ostentation |
| fortitude |
| temperament |
| exhibition |
| bravado |

Answers and Solutions to Exercise

1. dramatic
2. nullifies
3. vivacious
4. chaotic ... flaunt
5. lose
6. rationalize ... justifying ... advantageous
7. fundamental ... mundane ... catalyst for
8. exert
9. picturesque ... an exquisite
10. implications
11. preconceived ... an impoverished
12. fails ... inherently
13. sensitive to
14. dilapidated...high
15. sound ... belied
16. alternative
17. profession
18. polarized ... negligible ... deference
19. jaded ... indiscretions
20. precarious
21. growth ... fallen
22. austere
23. enigmatic
24. prejudice
25. drivel ... to entertain
26. integrate
27. immediacy ... pragmatism
28. advocating
29. protest ... overcrowding
30. neglectful
31. castigated ... stable
32. increased ... a loss
33. an anathema ... desirable
34. evil ... sophistication
35. reticent ... amiable
36. predisposition ... cataclysmic
37. menace ... non-ecofriendly
38. usefulness ... accepted
39. youthful
40. conflicting ... unequivocally
41. profiling ... influential
42. penchant ... matriarchal
43. tropical
44. rampaging ... irony
45. hyperbole
46. bravado

1. If the public expects a comedian to always make them laugh, then they might not accept a comedian in a serious role. Hence, the directors would be *loath* (reluctant) to cast a comedian in a dramatic role.

2. The phrase "all but" implies that the debate was a make-or-break event for the candidate. Suppose the candidate did well. Then his spirits would be high, and we would expect the missing word to be positive. However, a positive word in the phrase "*all but* _____ *any hope*" is awkward. Hence, the candidate must have done poorly in the debate and had his hopes for election nixed. So we turn to the answer-choices looking for "nixed." It's not there, but a synonym—*nullifies*—is.

3. Since no connecting word—such as *and, for, so*, etc.—follows the comma, the phrase "*seemingly with an endless reserve of energy*" defines the missing

word. Now, a person with an endless reserve of energy would be lively, which is the meaning of *vivacious*.

4. Recognize that the phrase "*dismantled by war and its development clogged by illiteracy*" is in apposition to the first blank. Such description would best be described as *chaotic*. The phrase "*In spite of*" lets us know that the locals do not feel how one would expect them to about their country. Thus, instead of feeling what we'd expect—disgrace—they take pride in their country, or *flaunt* their nationalism.

5. "Yet" draws a contrast between what one would expect an Atheist to do (renounce faith in God) and what Liharev did (maintained faith in God). In other words, he did not *lose* faith in God.

6. This is an example of a multiple blank question in which the answers heavily depend on each other. The sentence following the colon is in apposition to the sentence in front of it. For this question, perhaps the easiest blank to answer first is Blank 3, "_____ to him but injurious to others," which can be solved without referencing the rest of the sentence. "But" sets up a contradiction between "injurious" and the blank, which must mean "beneficial," or *advantageous*. Now, reread the entire sentence with "advantageous" in the blank. If someone is performing acts that help himself but hurt others, the first blank must mean something like "support." The word here, then, is *rationalize*. Reread the sentence with both blanks filled in. If a person is rationalizing evil, then they are "supporting"—or *justifying*—that belief system.

7. Start with the second blank. In the sentence structure—"drab, _____ DMV"—one can deduce that the blank is synonymous with "drab" — *mundane*. Now, turn to the third blank. The phrase "who would have believed" implies that the reality is the opposite of what one would expect. Now, one would not expect the drab DMV to be a *catalyst* for creativity. Return to the first sentence. If people are inspired by a drab location, then people's desire for expression must not come from the exterior, it must come from within—it is *fundamental*.

8. The sentence implies that even when Erikson knows he is taking the wrong path in life, he still cannot stop. That is, he cannot *exert* free will.

9. The sentence implies that the location, though having splendid natural settings, is distressed by the ongoing battle. We can observe from the structure of the sentence that both blanks explain the natural beauty of the location. The author implies that if the location had no overtones of the battlefield, it would have been a *picturesque* airfield in an *exquisite* part of the North.

10. The sentence is saying that although a word may not be explicitly sexist it may contain sexist connotations or *implications*.

11. One would reasonably assume, *preconceive*, that a state where parents are alleged to have sold their children in exchange for food is an *impoverished* state. Note, "impoverished" is the second-best choice for blank two. Although an impoverished state is probably impotent, impoverished describes the situation better.

12. Since man is violent, any useful theory of conflict resolution must incorporate this fact. Thus, any one that *fails* to account for it is *inherently* flawed.

13. The clause "whereas in a totalitarian regime, no one is listening" implies that a democracy does listen to protests. In other words, it is *sensitive to* protests.

14. "Although" sets up a contrast between what the property values are (*high*) and what one would expect them to be in a *dilapidated* (run down) community.

15. If the business were not sound, his irritability would *belie* (contradict) his claim that the business was *sound*.

16. The word "exhausted" implies that all other actions (*alternatives*) have been tried.

17. The sentence is pointing out that as a practical matter the legal *profession* pursues the truth through a rough and tumble path.

18. The second sentence contains the phrase "for example," indicating that it provides clarification for the previous sentence. An argument over where to place a comma, then, indicates that the subjects of debate are often *negligible* (insignificant). If sides are arguing merely to gain power over the other side, then politics have become *polarized*. Finally, if both sides are struggling for power, then they wouldn't give in—or show *deference* to the other side.

19. A financial scandal is an *indiscretion*; and it may not have made the front page because the public was *jaded* (worn out) by an excess of scandals.

20. The sentence is suggesting that it is risky—or *precarious*—to discuss certain subjects regardless of what you say.

21. "Although" sets up a contrast between what happened in the market over a two year period (*growth*) and what happened in some shorter periods during that time—it *fell*.

22. A complement is something that makes up a whole, bringing it to perfection. Of the answer-choices offered, only *austere* could complement "love" in such a manner.

23. We are told that the author is gracious, yet she makes the churlish comment: "My novels are to sophisticated for the American public." Such a comment would be considered *enigmatic*, as it is so out of her character.

24. "Nevertheless" points out a contrast in how the judge felt (*prejudice*) and how he acted (without prejudice).

25. "Condemnatory" implies that the word in the blank must mean something negative—*drivel*. The word "pretentious" indicates that the writer believes that the critics take themselves and movies too seriously. That is, the main purpose of a movie is merely *to entertain*.

26. Man is a social being; to function properly, he needs to be an integral part of society. When a person fails to *integrate* himself into society, he often feels alienated and incomplete, which, without a social support system, can lead to suicide. The author believes that those who commit suicide do so because they are unable to *integrate* themselves into the society.

27. According to the author, the core issue involves a hard, practical point that is to be dealt with a *pragmatic* approach. Pragmatism means "practical approach." The author stresses the *immediacy* of the situation since it is raising life-threatening issues.

28. The general is accusing the senator of being naive (unsophisticated) for believing—or *advocating*—that air strikes alone could stop the aggressors.

29. People are likely to *protest* a plan that they believe will cause gridlock. If they are protesting it, then, it must cause more negative effects, such as *overcrowding*.

30. "Though" sets up a contrast between "magnanimous" (charitable) and *neglectful*.

31. The sentence is implying that no one could have foreseen the collapse of the Soviet Union, so the intelligence community should not be criticized—or *castigated*—for also not foreseeing it. The author gives an example of an expert,

and if the author is defending the intelligence community, then the expert must not have foreseen it either, seeing it rather as a *stable* society.

32. In a shortage, fuel prices would *increase*. The sentence is pointing out, however, that in spite of the higher prices the suppliers saw a *loss* in profits.

33. The sentence is pointing out the difference between the attitudes of people in the '50s and the attitudes today. If Americans accept it today, then it used to be a curse—or *an anathema*—in the 50's. The opposite of a curse would be *desirable*.

34. The writer is pointing out that one who overcomes *evil* is more admirable than one who is born simple, lacking the *sophistication* to be bad.

35. If no peace treaty has been signed after 50 years, then the countries are probably *reticent* (reluctant) to develop more *amiable* (friendly) relations.

36. The author makes a distinction between two types of people who commit suicide—one type that can't bear tragic—or *cataclysmic*—events, and those who are born with an inclination—or *predisposition*—to commit suicide.

37. The second clause states that worldwide steps are being taken to ban plastic. The word "and" joining the two clauses of the sentence indicates that the first clause should provide a reason for the worldwide ban of plastic. The reason is that plastic is proving to be a *menace* to the environment. The second blank needs to be filled by a word that supports the statement and shows the negative consequences of plastic usage. The suitable word is *non-ecofriendly*.

38. The conjunction "and" in the phrase "Despite its _____ and safety" indicates that the missing word has a positive meaning because "safety" has a positive meaning. Since the sentence is implying that the drug is *useful* in curing depression and anxiety, it is expected that the drug would be widely used. But "despite" implies that the drug is not widely *accepted*.

39. The word "age" in the sentence implies that the missing word is characteristic of age. *Youthful* fits well: Despite her advanced age, she has a youthful sense of humor.

40. The word "and" in the phrase "different and _____ versions" indicates that the missing word is similar in meaning to the word "different." Now, different versions of an event can be *conflicting*. Furthermore, a dastardly act needs to be condemned *unequivocally*.

41. The show was organized to tell the stories of successful celebrities. By *profiling* these celebrities, the show narrates the stories of the *influential* newsmakers from all walks of life.

42. Since hyenas eat carrion (decaying flesh), they have an inclination—or *penchant*—for it. A society ruled by females is called *matriarchal*.

43. The word "both" in the statement implies there are two different types of sunscreen. Since one is internal, the other one should be external or at least of a different type. The choices "territorial," "atmospheric," "regional," and "polar" do not imply the opposite of internal. However, a "topical" treatment is applied to body surfaces, usually the skin. This is the opposite of internal treatment.

44. The first sentence describes AIDS as a big threat; it also describes another disease that is unreported and is on a greater *rampage*. Yet, the author says there is a cure for this silent killer. It is *ironic* that the silent killer causes more harm than AIDS, yet it is curable.

45. The statement implies that Michael is certainly not the greatest American actor but seems to Julianne by comparison. To believe him to be the greatest actor would be to indulge in *hyperbole*.

46. The word "only" in the first clause limits the meaning of courage: They have courage, but only to a point. The word "bluff" in the second clause indicates that their courage is merely bluster. This is the meaning of *bravado*.

www.ingramcontent.com/pod-product-compliance
Lightning Source LLC
Chambersburg PA
CBHW062008070426
42451CB00008BA/250